~ Dedication ~

I dedicate this book to my high school English teacher, Mrs. Shirley Fritz, Fairview High School, Farmer, Ohio, who influenced me as a youth between 1960-1965 to pursue my imagination and writing.

This page left blank

Table of Contents

INTRODUCTION

Thank you for purchasing this collection of 52 writing tips which I hope will help, guide and teach you different ways to improve your writing. So, how do you use this book? You could take each tip as a weekly lesson and apply it to your writing, reinforcing the tip on a daily basis for the week. Or you could just read all the tips and then attempt to apply them en masse to your current work.

This collection will delve into many facets of the writing spectrum including items such as tightening your writing, editing, expanding your creativity and understanding the craft.

Thinking INSIDE the Box

I hope you find this tip to be an interesting concept. We are always told to think *outside the box* but what really happens there? Exactly what is outside the box that you need to think about? We all have our comfort zone and I guess that is what others are considering the box. Maybe we don't have to go outside the box but learn to look in the other corners of the current box you're in. Maybe you're just looking at a blank wall of the box... so learn to scrutinize the corners.

Today I'm going to help you learn how to do that by showing you how to think, or at least see things differently.

First, let me say there are NO wrong answers!

Step 1) Above you see 4 items: A horse, a seahorse, a rose and a shark. Select the two which you feel are the most closely related.

Step 2) Think about why you chose the two. What is the common connection you feel binds them together?

Now let's evaluate possible answers and scenarios.

1) Most people will probably select seahorse/shark. Why? Ocean, aquatic, fish.

2) Some will pick horse/seahorse. Why? Equine or the 'horsy' concept; more later.

3) Horse/rose? How about the Kentucky Derby?

4) Horse/shark? Both can bite.

5) Rose/shark or rose/seahorse? Alphabetical? Deadly? Ethereal?

As I stated earlier, there are no wrong answers but each answer is a little peek into your mindset and how you think.

#1 is a mature, educated choice.

#2 is how a child would see the connection of horses.

#3 is the mindset of a gambler

#4 is probably somebody who has a fear or phobia of being bitten. Afterall, shark bites are terrifying and a person who is not familiar with horses might consider those large teeth quite fearful.

#5 is very abstract to see an alphabetical sequence (R/S) or to even consider the water in which sharks and seahorses live as being deadly to roses. Roses are considered a delicate flower and seahorses tend to be that rare creature — both of them almost ethereal in their existence.

What does this all mean? How does it pertain to your writing? It depends on your mindset...

#1 is for adult writing where maturity and education is needed.

#2 is the mindset of a child, horsies. A writer of children's books needs to think as a child.

#3 shows you inside the mind of a gambler; a character who sees winning potential everywhere.

#4 displays fears; again a characteristic to endow upon your hero/heroine.

#5 is necessary for the quirkiness of your tale, to keep your reader involved.

So, now you are in the box and you've been looking at the corners. Most people just know the corner they are sitting in (Seahorse/Shark or Horse/Seahorse) yet for a writer, to be inside the mind of your character, you have to know what they are thinking... not what YOU are thinking.

Want to try another one? No pictures this time, just words.

1) Horse

2) 4-leaf Clover

3) Horse Shoe

4) Garden

Yes, the obvious is horse/horse shoe but then again, there is horse/4-leaf clover (gambling or feeding), horse/garden (a farm), 4-leaf clover/garden (growing), horse shoe/4-leaf clover (luck) and horse-shoe/garden (plowing).

Amazing how the mind works! Now I challenge YOU to look into that corner and find a different perspective on a view you've been staring at for the last few days. Look beyond the obvious and try to see the world through the eyes of your character.

WEEK 2:

That As•Ing•Ly ~ Editing Tricks

You've just finished the G.A.N — Great American Novel — and are ready to have it professionally edited. You've checked it over at least four or maybe even upwards of twelve times. All the glaring errors are missing, spelling is correct and the punctuation is perfect, as is the dialogue.

You send your baby off. Now, you patiently wait for the package to come back, and it does. Eagerly you rip open the envelope and look to see what glowing accolades the editor has for your work.

Horrors! This can't be!

There are hundreds... no, thousands of red marks all over the pages. Every page is riddled with small, red "X" marks, red words, red scribble lines. Red is everywhere!

Tears well up. You swoon into your chair and gently pat your chest, hoping your heart beat will return to normal. Finally you brave the beast and place your sacred, yet recently desecrated, tome on the desk and slowly read the editor's notes and begin to scan the corrections made.

Interesting terminology, you think.

"That" is a fluff word. You read your sentence aloud, with and without the "that" word. "I received a note that you wanted to see me." You read the next sentence where the word is crossed out. "He knew perfectly well that I could hear his thoughts." Slowly your head nods in understanding approval. "That" is a fluff word. You glance through the remainder of the page; seven times. The next page reveals six, followed by another 8 on page 3. Counting the first ten pages you find "that" scratched out over fifty times. Your mind goes into overdrive as it calculates an average. Two hundred and forty three pages times five... it equals... you gasp at the shock! Over twelve hundred words lost in this novel.

Panic twists your stomach and you flinch at the thought. When you flipped through the pages, there were some with a large, red "X" on them. That could be hundreds of more words lost. You gulp a glass of water to quench the sudden dryness in your throat and then take deep slow breaths and slowly count to ten.

Your eyes notice the next correction; a crossed out 'as if' in the middle of a sentence. "Alone in each of our separate locations, it would appear as if we were talking to the trees."

There is no 'as if' in the scene described. You were talking to the trees from an observer's viewpoint. If somebody were to see you talking, alone, perhaps facing a tree, there is no reason for an 'as if' in the sentence. WYSIWYG. That's right... *What You See Is What You Get*.

You move to the next 'as' correction. "Rynlon needed to be as courteous, however relevant the action was." Again, a superfluous word added. You note there are three 'as' corrections on this page and do some quick mental math. Another almost one thousand words lost.

The next correction you notice is a group of circled words. First is 'Struggling' with a line to 'Holding,' line connected to 'Chancing,' line connected to 'Knowing,' line connected to 'Seeing,' line connected to 'Going' finally connected to 'Holding.' You see the note in the margin with a line to the connected words. "This is what I refer to as the 'ing' syndrome. These seven sentences all begin with an 'ing' word and becomes quite monotonous reading. The sentences usually start with three or four words followed by a comma and then some action which can always be made into a separate line. *Turning the page, I saw Betty enter the room*. Now exactly what is true here? You can only see Betty when you turn the page? Would you have seen Betty if you hadn't turned the page? Was Betty part of the page and that is why you saw her? The fix? Delete the first three words and comma. Unfortunately, it is rather bland, isn't it? So learn to write better. *When I finished reading the page and began to turn it, I looked up and noticed Betty walk into the library*. Originally, you had nine words. Delete three? Down to six. Ah, but re-write and now you have twenty-one words and a better structured sentence with more body and detail.

Again you nod your head with approval and slide to the next correction: adverbial dialogue. "*I wish he would notice me,*" *Becky said longingly*. You follow the line to another side note which says: If you show us she is mooning over him, you don't need to use an adverbial modifier. *Becky followed him with her eyes while he walked across the room. She exhaled loudly in a sigh*. "*I wish he would notice me,*" *she whispered*. A good author shows, not tells.

You notice the number of adverbial errors and realize more lost words, but reluctantly note you have the potential to increase word count in the showing of the story.

If you are thinking the above is only for the G.A.N., you're wrong; it's not. It also applies to the short stories and articles you write. Publishers are looking for tight, well written pieces. It doesn't mean just a good plot; it means tight, well written exposition. Let me show you a secret about the bottom line. Using the 'that' error from above, let's assume a few details.

Scenario: A short story of 9,000 words = 30 pages X 5 'that' per page = 150 superfluous words

• You submitted 9000 words to markets @ $.10, $.05, $.03 and received rejects, no sales.

• 9000 words X $.02 = $180.00 ~ this is the sale you accepted at a low rate.

• IF you had cleaned up the story, wrote tighter with only 150 'that' errors removed.

• 8850 words X $.10 = $885.00 ~ this is a potential high rate.

• 8850 words X $.05 = $442.50 ~ another high rate.

• 8850 words X $.03 = $265.50 ~ just ONE penny more than your sale.

Usually higher payments indicate a better known market and therefore a kudos for your byline. An article sold to "Boy's Life" is more impressive than "Bob's Online Gazette" to your next prospective publisher.

So, in conclusion, when you finally realize *that as•ing•ly* can make a difference not only in a tighter, well written novel but also in a better, tighter short story or article, you will suddenly find a larger, well deserved payment. You're the writer; you decide.

Character Descriptions

Within the pages of your story, you invite the reader to meet your characters and get to know them as interesting and complex individuals with needs, desires, talents, and shortcomings. It is this mixture of components that attracts us to certain characters, repels us from others, leaves us neutral regarding some of them or even worse, disinterested. How do we get those aspects and properties of each character across using only the written word? How do we then further inspire the reader to absorb those characteristics, and create the mental image you're attempting to project?

As writers of any type of genre, if we don't get all that we want onto the pages, we have not done our jobs effectively, nor satisfactorily. While all readers will see in their minds unique variations of the worlds we've created, there should be some threads of constancy from one reader to the next. When a reader finishes one of my stories, I know that each one will have a unique flavor, so I am not shocked or disappointed when someone tells me something different from another. Sometimes I am pleasantly surprised by their creativity and ingenuity in discovering some aspect I did not imagine. But overall, they should each produce the same basic story, and provide the same overall experience.

Even when using the same recipe, each cook's final result will resemble all the others, but each final result will possess individuality. Temperature, humidity, altitude, and quality of water will affect the dish, along with the cook's individual methods, tools and measuring acuity.

So, how do you describe a character without breaking the action of your novel or sounding like you're writing a profile on a dating form? I offer five options.

1. Describe with action, dialogue tags, or simple dialogue to detail what your characters are wearing. You don't need a paragraph about what they are wearing, unless fashion is extremely important to the plot. You can work descriptions in easily. For example: *Before Jessica could finish telling Jack she loved having dinner with him, the waiter tripped and spilled red wine down her blue, silk blouse.* That method is much better than instead of writing: *Jessica wore a blue, silk blouse on her date.*

2. Write about a couple of physical traits. You don't need to describe every single body part—as stated before, this is not a dating

profile. Here's an example that will give readers a picture about Jessica: *Jessica pulled her curly, blonde hair into a ponytail to show off her small ears, highlighted with diamond stud earrings.* Or for a different image: *Jessica ran her fingers through her purple and orange, spiked hair before putting in her nose ring.*

3. I wrote a young adult novel about a 15 year old boy named Donnie who just happens to be a nervous teenager, but I don't come out and tell the reader that fact. I showed his nervousness by describing his actions: sweaty armpits, scratching or playing with his hair, chewing a fingernail and constantly strumming his fingers on any surface. Is your character energetic? What traits can you give him to show this? Think about ways to describe what your character is like without telling the reader.

4. I also used dialogue to describe Donnie. You can do this easily. Is your character from a certain part of the United States (pop or soda, bag or sack) or world (toilet, bathroom, loo)? Think about the vocabulary your character uses or the way he or she talks. Donnie is a nervous teenager, so he talks really fast with long, run on sentences full of adjectives. Yes, even the speed of speech can be described.

5. Your character has hobbies, family, and friends. Use these to describe your character, too. Donnie idolizes John Wayne because his mom, who is deceased, had a collection of Wayne memorabilia and grew up in a home that was only two doors down from where John Wayne was born. This shows Donnie is unique and also that he misses his mom. I don't come out and state the obvious in my description. I show it with his hobbies, conversations and interactions with other family members and friends.

Building A Believable Character

Exactly what is a "Believable Character" and why is it so important to you, the writer?

If your character is banal, transparent or utterly lackluster, your reader will quickly lose interest in the story. That doesn't mean the person has to be a super-hero or bigger-than-life; but every main character in your story needs to be able to stand on their own merits.

Is a believable character easy to develop? No! It is not easy. It takes creative imagination to develop characters who can strike a chord inside your reader and can identify with or embrace that character. You want the reader to care about what happens. You want the reader's gut to drop out of their body when your character falls into the chasm.

So exactly what does this mean? I finished reading Melanie Rawn's "Dragon Prince" and "Dragon Star" series; her characters came alive and everyone existed inside my mind. I kept turning the pages to find out what would happen next. Were the characters real? Yes and no. They weren't real in the sense they actually existed but yes, they were real within my mind and definitely during the moments I was inside the world Ms. Rawn created. I cared. I was emotionally involved with their lives and happenings so that when one character died, I actually had tears welling in my eyes. I felt as though I'd lost a very dear friend. Melanie Rawn had grabbed my very being with that particular character, connecting with my soul and spirit. It was then I realized, if I want to be a writer, I need to do the same for my readers.

Try some of these characters: Tom Sawyer, Indiana Jones, Hercule Poirot, Dracula, Harry Potter, or Heidi. Those names evoked images in your mind and you were reminded of a scene, a line, or a tidbit involving them. They were believable characters and that means you remembered them.

You need more than physical features for a character such as eye and hair color, height, weight, skin tone and texture, sex, species, scars, likes and dislikes, etc. etc. etc. ad nauseam.

Characters need reality and emotion. Each person has weaknesses and strengths. Lock those down in your character, bring them to the reader's attention but remember these can and should change as your story progresses. Weaknesses such as a fear should be overcome or at least challenged. The reader needs to see emotions such as anger and aggression. Don't just describe them, show them. "*She stomped across the room with fists tightly clenched.*" versus "*She angrily moved across the room.*" The first sentence really brings out the image while the second is rather bland.

Think of it this way — If your character was raised in a nunnery, she shouldn't be shifting her hip to one side, placing her hand on it, chewing and snapping some gum, fluffing her hair and nasally quipping a line like a mobster's moll.

If the character has a 'nunnery upbringing' one would visualize a 'nice' girl with appropriate attire, manners and actions, not some desperate housewife. If this character has fallen from grace, you need to show the transition from being a good girl.

Remember, show, don't tell. Develop your character. Which of the two following described characters do you enjoy?

Example 1: *Bob stood five foot, ten inches tall unless his hair was disheveled, then he stood five foot, almost eleven inches. He had blue eyes, blond hair and enjoyed sports. His wife's name is Henrietta and they had played tennis today. He kissed her.*

Example 2: *Bobby sprinted across the tennis court to join his wife, Henrietta. It had been an energetic game today, his blue eyes sparkled and she tousled his blond hair as he towered over her at five foot, ten inches and kissed the top of her head.*

Each of the above examples used the same basic information. Which do I prefer? I think Bobby sounds like a lot of fun and I now know that Henrietta is much shorter than him. Sorry, but Bob reads like an accounting ledger.

If you don't like your character, you can almost bet the farm that your reader isn't going to enjoy the character, either.

Secondary Characters aka Walk-on Characters

We've all had to do it, as an author you need to write them. I'm discussing those characters who come alive in your story for a brief moment then disappear into obscurity. Perhaps they may make another appearance, more than likely not.

There are volumes of books on how to build a character, how to define a character, make your lead character memorable, etc etc. but how many of them touch on the non-main characters?

Today I'm going to talk about secondary characters.

To begin, exactly how much description do you, the writer, add to this person?

Simple answer: as much as you want.

If you've ever attended a theater and watched a live performance, you may see a walk-on person who only comes in and places a glass of water on the table before disappearing stage left. How many times has a star been upstaged by a non-talking person? Don't even attempt to answer that question. Does the person move in a way that is noticeable? Perhaps a stiff walk, slight goose-stepping, or maybe the person bends over dramatically to place the glass precisely in the middle of the table, using their fingers to snap away some unseen dust. In other words, they don't just walk in, plunk down the glass of water, and walk off. They do it with panache.

There is nothing wrong with writing secondary characters to have some flair, some distinctive detail to allow your reader to enjoy not only the main characters, but also those who are making the main characters great. My son had multiple parts in a musical – *Joseph and the Amazing Technicolor Coat* – and really hammed up a scene as one of Joseph's brothers. He didn't have a talking part for that scene, but people remembered him. How? While standing there with the other non-descriptive brothers, he decided to scratch his butt. No, not a little finger itch, he used his hand and moved his robe so people could see he was really digging for that scratch. He pulled that during rehearsal as a joke— the director loved it and that little action stayed in for all five showings of the high school play. After the shows, when asked which brother he portrayed, he'd reply with 'The one who itched.' and everyone knew who he was.

11

So how do you do this supposed magic? How do you get away with making secondary characters come alive? Again, it's a very simple step.

Example 1: *The butler walked stiffly into the room, glanced haughtily down his nose at the seated group, announced dinner, performed an excellent 'about-face' and left.*

You've done your job and given a walk-on character a description and a personality. In this particular instance, the butler didn't do it and will perhaps only make one more small entrance later on in the story. I can hear you screaming 'cop out' with an easy example. True, but I'm sure you could feel the ooze of disdain and his snappy, business attitude.

To help, the following is more descriptive. Setup: Sort of a 'House on the Prairie' type setting with Betsy (our lead) and her friends in a store buying candy; they depart. (Note: the following is not properly formatted with paragraphs, etc.)

Example 2: *Old Barry wedged the legs of the ladder into the store's porch floor then leaned it against the porch roof post. He wiggled the ladder to make sure it wouldn't move. Betsy and her cluster of girlfriends rushed by him as he started up the rungs. The sun now beamed brightly after the rain shower and Betsy immediately raised a hand to shade her eyes; she didn't see the on-coming wagon. The mud splattered up as the wheels dropped into the collected water puddles near her and Betsy immediately began screaming. In her shock, Betsy's hand came up tossing her bag of candy over her head, back toward Old Barry. "Mr. Bashore, just look at my new Sunday dress," she screamed at the passing wagon-master. "Do you have any idea what my mama is going to say?" Her girlfriends, safely behind her a few steps when it happened, now hovered about Betsy, attempting to help remove the larger clumps of mud. Old Barry was startled by the flying assortment of candy, lost balance and fell off the ladder, snagging his overalls on one rail of the ladder. He dangled in mid-air struggling to set himself free, his feet just mere inches from the floor. Betsy again looked down at her wet dress covered in mud and started to cry. Suddenly Beth Ann started to snicker, putting a gloved hand to her lips. Betsy got mad. Then Elizabeth began to giggle. Betsy got madder. Her beautiful dress was muddy and her best friends were laughing—she was not amused. Jane finally joined in the amusement and was laughing just as hard as the other two girls. Betsy fumed. She didn't like being laughed at, stamped her foot, tossed her head, shaking her long curly tresses and began to walk away from them.*

"Look, Betsy," Beth Ann said and pointed to Old Barry struggling to free himself. The ladder was clearly wedged between the post of the porch and the porch's deck. Mr. Peterson ran out of his store wiping his hands on his green apron. He carefully pulled the ladder toward him so Old Barry could free himself. Betsy glanced at the scene, turned and walked away. It didn't matter to her what that old fool did. Her friends quickly joined her but she remained silent.

In the above example there were a couple of walk-on characters. The main character, Betsy is obviously very self-centered and/or spoiled. Her friends have been in the story so they've been pretty much described before. Old Barry is a new character and has a brief moment of limelight to add a little levity to Betsy's traumatic mudding. Mr. Peterson has an even smaller part. You probably visualized Old Barry wearing baggy overalls with over-the-shoulder straps, an old floppy hat and he probably even had a scraggly beard. A likeable old fart. Somehow I saw Mr. Peterson as tall, with a green apron (as stated), so he probably had on a starched, white shirt and my mind also showed him with thinning hair parted down the center.

Note I added hair, clothes colors and height in my mind just with a simple "Mr. Peterson ran out of his store wiping his hands on his green apron." If you give the reader 'some' detail, their mind will fill in the rest to round out the character. If I had used the term 'huffed' rather than 'run' – I probably would have envisioned a heavier, more robust man. Amazing what one word can do to a description.

Even a 'mob' can be secondary characters. To say something like "*The mob stood there watching the parade.*" is very banal and boring. To begin with, a mob is a collection of people who are actively doing something. Otherwise, you have a group. In other words "The group stood there watching the parade." How about "*The mob jeered and whistled as the parade passed them.*" See? The mob is actively doing something. The group is watching.

So, in closing, the secondary cast, those walk-on people who aren't the main characters, don't have to be relegated to non-descriptive parts, they can have charisma, personality and definition to become, and be a part of your memorable story.

WEEK 6:

Sabotaging Character Believability

There is more to writing than just making sure how your character appears flawless with great descriptions and snappy dialogue. Read the following three small passages and see if you can figure out the problem with your character.

Example #1:

Jeff placed a foot in the stirrup and lifted himself onto the horse's back.

"Are you leaving already?" Becky whined.

Three quick steps and he embraced her once again.

"Should I really leave?" Jeff whispered.

Example #2:

Grabbing the broadsword with both hands he glared at the on-coming dwarf. The princess had to be defended. His left hand gently pushed the princess behind him for protection as he lunged with the sword held tightly between his hands.

Example #3:

Brad nodded then winked, his bright blue eyes glistened in the sunlight.

"Do you think we should do this?" Henry asked. "This is going to hurt."

"Just put your back into it and we should be okay," Brad replied. He placed a shoulder against the large, abrasive stone, pushed and winced. Tears flowed from his dark eyes. "It just has to work," Brad grunted.

The above are subtle errors. What were they?

Example #1: If your character is on a horse, exactly how does he do three quick steps? Does he float through the air? Always know where your character is.

Example #2: How many hands does the swordsman have, assuming him to be human? If he is holding the sword with two hands he can't use another to protect the princess.

14

Example #3: Brad has what color eyes? Bright blue? Remember the wink? So later, can they really be dark?

You have to be an actor. When you write a scene, step through the dialogue, the actions and the emotions. You'll quickly realize the impossibilities. If he is on a horse, he can't walk. If she is scared out of her wits, I'm pretty sure she won't be running willy-nilly around a musty basement of a deserted, haunted house. How I would love to make a comment about those who write ... shall we say exotic erotica? Let me put it this way—I was in the Navy for five years and read novels like J. R. R. Tolkien's *Lord of the Rings*, but many of my shipmates actually read "other literature" while out at sea and I would hear them say something to the effect of "No frigging way could they do that!" or "That's a total physical impossibility in that position." Permitting such actions to happen allows your believable character to fall on his or her face in your reader's eyes. The more real your characters are in the reader's mind, the more believable they become. Any instance that makes the reader stop and think or falters their thought process, you lose that reader. They have dropped out of the world you've created.

Remember, actors don't change personas, features, personalities and traits in the blink of an eye unless they are putting in contact lens, wearing a wig, or are mildly schizophrenic.

You'd best be acting out that scene; making sure that even if your character is a contortionist, is that position remotely feasible? If you drop a reader out of your created world, THEY REMEMBER!

Paraphrasing Victor Melling [Michael Caine] from "Miss Congeniality" who said: You *wear* the crown, *be* the crown, you *are* the crown!

*You *think* the character, *act* the character – you *are* the character.*

Alien Sex or What To Do When Your Partner Isn't Human

Sure, you've just finished watching one of the popular sci-fi shows and there was a scene where one of the regular cast had a pseudo sensual love scene with a quasi-human. His arms enwrapped about her body, their lips locked in an intimate moment of bliss and face to face they are having that almost love session. Better than 99% of all alien contact involving sex will be of a heterosexual nature with either species offering the male or female as the participants.

Have you noticed that most aliens are usually pretty humanoid? Ever wondered why? Easy. A sex scene between a human and some sort of hybrid aardvark octopus gets too difficult. Not necessarily awkward to write, but too complicated to convey in words.

It is our mind set. We can visualize a scene inside our brain but can't get the proper words to explain the intricacies of octopus suckers, tentacles and an aardvark nose and tongue melding with our human counterpart. I apologize, perhaps some may be able to imagine that.

Of course, sex doesn't have to be necessarily with a space type alien. There are many other types that can be included in the mix: fairies, demons, robots, ghosts, Sasquatch, mermaids, and the list goes on.

Again, this list of possible love gods/goddesses will be nearly humanoid and have the corresponding sexual anatomy necessary for the love scene. This is where the art of writing and imagination can delve into the depths of wonder. This is where the alien doesn't need to be human in their sexuality.

What does this mean? Sex doesn't necessarily need to be the act as humans normally relate. Remember the movie "Cocoon" and the sex scene between Earthman Steve Guttenberg and Antarean Tahanee Welch in the pool? Steve experienced one heck of a sensation at Tahanee's sharing of herself with him. Another instance would be "Starman" with Jeff Bridges and Karen Allen. Again, somehow, even though it is not fully explained, Karen becomes pregnant and is carrying his child.

Back in 1983 there was a television series entitled "V" about visitors from space. It revolved around aliens coming to our planet. There were a few angles involving romance between these aliens and us. In fact, one story theme was about a young human girl and her alien boyfriend and their offspring.

Even if your non-human character is of the fanciful, demonic or mythological, the act itself can be described beyond the realms of mere mortals. Perhaps your mermaid and sailor can mate in the swirling waves of the ocean, your demon and innocent maiden make love in the throes of a fiery passion pit, or a leprechaun, by eating mushrooms, can become full sized to exercise his manly acts. Use your imagination to give your non-human creation the best possible sex.

Now exactly how sensual and sexual the science fiction and/or fantasy story gets is each writers own decision. Usually, in non-erotic type genres of sci-fi and fantasy, sex, the act itself, is normally downplayed with the strategy of foreplay getting most of the attention. I am not saying the story should be sanitized of sex but only if the act itself is important to the plot do you need to let your reader's libido run rampant. This is true of almost any element in the story—it must promote the plot or storyline.

Sex is the interlude and is best left to the imagination of the reader; build it up and then bask in the aftermath of the moment. Your reader can fill in the blanks if they know what it is about or left as blanks if the reader is too young to comprehend.

Afterglow: the Real Power Behind
A Literary Sexual Encounter
by Mitchel Whitington

Afterglow may sound like some component of a romance novel, and it usually is, but it is also one of the most powerful elements of a written sex scene. Simply defined, afterglow is the activity that occurs immediately following the sexual encounter. Your characters may be cuddling, kissing, arguing, or leaving - you may find out that the sex itself isn't as important in your story as what happens afterward! It is your chance to give the readers a deep, personal insight to the characters involved. That's easy to state outright, but the best way to understand the power of afterglow is to look at a few scenes that use it. For example, consider the case of two characters, Matthew and Alison. They've just made love, and the scene picks up...

With a slow, deliberate motion Matthew rolled over. He was lying next to Alison, their bodies touching, their deep breathing almost in synch.

She smiled, exhaled, and whispered, "My God, was that great, or what? Matthew, you are magnificent."

Matthew sat up and swatted her on the thigh. "So the ladies tell me, doll. You see the zapper for the TV over there?"

Glancing around the room, he picked up a remote control off of the nightstand and snapped the television to life. With only a few clicks, a football game filled the screen. "Damn! They're only into the first quarter, and Dallas is already behind!" He pulled a cigarette from a pack beside the bed, lit it with his sterling silver lighter shaped like a woman's body, and exhaled a cloud of smoke into the room. Without missing a single play on the screen, he took another drag and said, "Hey, why don't you make yourself useful and go get me a beer?"

Alison stared at the ceiling for a moment, heaved a sigh, and rolled out of bed to fetch his request.

He cut his eyes over sharply. "Hey, don't cop an attitude just because I want to catch the game. Don't worry, I'll do you again at half time. By the way, when we're done, you're gonna have to take a cab home. I feel like drinking some serious beer tonight, and I don't want to get busted out on the road."

"Wonderful." Alison plodded toward the kitchen.

Don't you have a strong opinion about Matthew at this point? How about Alison, putting up with his attitude and behavior? Keep those opinions in mind, but consider a slightly different ending to the same love scene...

With a slow, deliberate motion Matthew rolled over. He was lying next to Alison, their bodies touching, their deep breathing almost in synch.

She smiled, exhaled, and whispered, "My God, was that great, or what? Matthew, you are magnificent."

Matthew sat up and touched her gently on the thigh. He looked into her eyes for what seemed like an eternity, and then in a low, soft voice said, "I'll be right back."

He disappeared through the bedroom's doorway, while she lay there staring blissfully at the ceiling. In only a moment, he appeared again. His left hand was balancing a wooden tray with two fluted glasses and a bowl overflowing with strawberries. In his other he held a bottle of French Champagne. "I thought that a few accessories to the evening might be in order."

Setting the tray on the bed, he stroked her hair, then poured them each a glass of the sparkling wine. "Just something to get our energy back up." He handed the glass to her, and softly clinked his against it. "I also brought some fruit for a snack."

Taking a strawberry in his fingers, he touched it against her lips, then trailed it slowly down her neck. "Oh, and if we're going to be drinking this wine, it might be wise for us to stay indoors." He reached out and kissed her forehead. "I'm afraid that you're going to have to stay here for the evening." Matthew lightly drew the strawberry between her breasts, and continued downward.

"Wonderful," she gasped, then lay back and closed her eyes.

You come away from this second scene with a much different idea about Matthew and Alison, even though the fact that they had sex didn't change. As you might be able to tell, no matter how much forethought and detail you put into the actual description of the coupling between the two characters, they can be defined in greater detail by their actions when the big event is over.

But don't add an intimate encounter in your story just for the heck of it - think of a sex scene much like you'd think of a backgammon game between two characters. Just like there's no good reason to have two characters sit down and play an ordinary game of backgammon without explanation, there's probably no good reason for them just to have sex - unless you can use it to further the plot or develop the characters. An ordinary backgammon game becomes very important if an argument ensues afterwards, and one character shoots another with a .44 magnum. By the same token, a sex scene is crucial to your story if you use it correctly - and afterglow is the perfect mechanism to employ. To carry the comparison even further, if you were having trouble writing all the drawn-out details of the backgammon game, it would be enough to set the game in motion, then pick it up at the interesting part after the game. The same applies to sex scenes!

Many writers are intimidated by writing about the mechanics of sex - I know that I am. Most of the scenes that I've tried to detail sound like something right out of Penthouse Forum: "Carrie screamed loudly as Rodger thrust his throbbing missile of love into her silky passage of warmth..." Well, you get the idea. The turnaround in my crafting of intimate scenes occurred when I attended a session on romance writing at a conference where the entire focus was "afterglow."

As the speaker wove her tales, I immediately saw the potential power in the prose. After all, the moments immediately following the lovemaking session are when the characters are most vulnerable, completely raw. They've just shared the ultimate personal experience with each other, so all pretense is stripped aside. What happens? Does the guy fall asleep, the girl start to cry, or do the two catch their breath and go at it again? Anything is possible, but the one fact that is certain is that their behavior will expand the reader's view of their character.

If you're having trouble writing your sex scene, just leave out the act itself! Get them into bed, or onto the kitchen floor, or in the front seat of the 18-wheeler, and give the reader a sentence or two to let them know what is happening. From that point, jump to the afterglow scene and start working your literary magic.

Think back to the two examples at the start of this article. In the first one, it would be extremely easy to picture Matthew going out to rob a convenience store later - he just seems like that sort of fellow. Would the second-article Matthew do that? Of course not! In fact, you probably wouldn't be surprised to learn that he later revealed that he had written a love poem for Alison. And in the first example, why in the world would Alison put up with such behavior from her lover? If I were to act like that after a romantic interlude with my wife, I'd find myself sleeping out in the back yard. Perhaps that version of Alison has a weakness that she has to overcome later in the story.

There are a thousand ways to portray the same two characters in the exact same situation. Their actions not only told you more about them, but also painted a mental image of the surroundings that they were in. In the first example, you probably envisioned the pair in a cheap apartment. The scene for the second Matthew/Alison in your mind's eye was most likely a lush, romantically lit bedroom with candles all around. Let's look at one more alternative to the scene:

With a slow, deliberate motion Matthew rolled over. He was lying next to Alison, their bodies touching, their deep breathing almost in synch.

She smiled, exhaled, and whispered, "My God, was that great, or what? Matthew, you are magnificent."

Matthew rolled into a ball, and put his fist against his mouth. "It was okay, then, Madame?" he asked timidly.

Alison sat up, stood, then straightened her leather corset with a loud snap. "Oh, it was fine, Matthew. But I would think that the CEO of a Fortune 500 company could do much, much better." She snatched a riding crop from the nightstand, and stuck him sharply across his thigh.

"Mistress Alison!" Matthew gasped in pain, "Please!"

"Oh, it's going to be a long evening for you, my little executive. I hope that you are planning on spending the night here in my dungeon."

Matthew drew into a fetal position, and whimpered, "Yes, Mistress. As you command."

"Wonderful." Alison smiled confidently, and selected a wooden paddle from the implements hanging on the wall.

I've used the same basic setting - the conclusion of two people having sex - for three completely different scenes, and in each one you get a very definitive feel for the characters. Never once did I describe the mechanics of the sexual encounter, yet in the afterglow scene you had a preconceived notion about it by the time you finished reading.

Afterglow is that powerful — quit worrying about writing sex, and use its afterglow as a mighty tool in your writing!

About the Author: Mitchel Whitington is an author and speaker - visit Mitchel's website at http://www.whitington.com/write/articles.htm.

WEEK 9:

Writing & Politics: Parallel Worlds of Perception

The dimensions of writing and politics are filled with illusions based on our, the voters, perceptions. We seek our readers' votes when we ask them to purchase our work whether it is a small article or major opus. In the same manner the politician seeks to win our votes at the poll by molding our opinions of both himself and his platform, we must remain friendly, treat our public with respect, and never insult their intelligence.

Although it is true, like the politician, we tend to manipulate our worlds to our liking. But unlike the greedy politician, a good writer gives his reader what he seeks, truths that will leave him stronger for his journey. Nevertheless, perception is much more than a marketing ploy or a clever sales campaign. Our process of manipulating should begin long before the book reaches the printer or the bookstores' shelves.

While writing, a skilled writer uses metaphors, similes, and hyperbole to aid the reader to visualize a setting and make the scene come alive. We labor night and day to pluck the choicest action verbs and the best descriptive nouns to paint a wind-tossed palate of color, taste, smell, sound and texture on the backdrop of our reader's experiences. These are all elements of perception.

While we must remain vigilant against preaching, neither can we afford to lock the doors to our souls and morals to keep our audience at an arm's length from our feelings. Emotion is the elixir our reader's thirst for most; the ability to climb inside the point-of-view character and feel his adrenalin induced heart pumping. That is why they buy our books, or ravenously consume our short stories. Those doors, no matter how much we might wish to keep them bolted, must remain open for those who'd seek the deepest meanings behind our stories. That inquiring reader must be free to perceive our innermost feelings, while drawing on emotions of his own.

Politicians graciously sidestep issues rather than face obstacles. Although you may choose to misdirect the reader's attention away from key elements vital to your plot, never lie or deceive him. If you do, he will feel betrayed by your mistrust. For instance, if the protagonist kills the rapist in her kitchen with a meat cleaver, it would be ideal, somewhere earlier, to show her chopping vegetables with a kitchen knife which was hanging beside the cleaver. By the conclusion the reader may have forgotten the nasty weapon dangling from the brass hook over the island of cabinets where the rapist corners the housewife. Nevertheless, the reader will feel inwardly satisfied he was given all the facts. The reader should know all the relevant details the POV character learns as he uncovers them.

Your fan must remain free to witness and temporarily live within your created world through your character's eyes; perception is the key. To do this, a writer must understand how humans view their environment. When you enter an airport, do you notice details like the countless businessmen wearing suits and toting briefcases? Do you notice the hundreds of vacationing families? If you do, it is more as swarms of noisy crickets rather than as individuals. It is far more likely the bearded vagrant dressed in rags and carrying a cardboard box strung and held together with red ribbon would grab your attention. Upon entering the mob boss's office, is it more likely your hero would notice the neatly arranged oak desk or the laser scar over his scowling bodyguard's remaining gunmetal-gray eye? What we notice most is the unusual, the out of place, so your character must view his surroundings in this realistic light.

No matter how much you might despise the political axiom, remember: in the world of writing, like in politics, truth is perception.

Sparky: A New Angle On an Old Story

Many times when a story comes to mind you really don't know what the final market will be. This was the case of "Sparky" that I put together mentally a long time ago and kept playing with over the years... and I do mean years. I guess my reluctance in putting "Sparky" on paper was due to my ignorance of a possible paying market. I usually attempt to ascertain the "where it will sell" before I write. Still, even after the original was on paper, it was shoved into a file folder and relegated to an unmarked grave in my desk drawer. So, here's the story:

# # # # #

Sparky

There he goes again, shooting across a galaxy. Sparky just couldn't control himself. Give him a few million miles of open space and off he'd go.

Of course, what would you expect from a young upstart? Sparky was only nearing his 15th century, quite youthful in the scheme of the cosmos.

"Mrs. Way," the ominous voice boomed. "Once again your son has strayed."

She quickly assessed the situation and could see Sparky moving between Alpha Centauri and Epsilon 6.

"I'm sorry, God," she replied. "He's really a very good boy, just a little rambunctious and hyperactive."

"Well, I've been meaning to talk to you about him," the voice said. "We've got to find a way of controlling that rascal."

"I'm open to suggestions." Eons of worry weighed on her words. "For the last few centuries I've tried to keep a reign on his route, but," the remainder of her words were consumed by the silent void of space.

"Last week Miss Saturn complained he flew by her so fast she still hasn't been able to gain control of her ring alignments." God sighed. "Yesterday Nebula 2A6E caught him buzzing the smaller asteroids of Stellar Xarg 216."

Miss Milky Way considered the consequences of Sparky's actions. She remembered what had happened to Regis Comet when he went renegade and kept orbiting recklessly. The stars in her hair bobbled when she shook her head at the memory. That's all Regis Comet was; a memory. The rule was simple. "Live within your assigned orbit."

"Sparky," God called.

The young star stopped dead in his tracks, his excess radiation flaring in a corona around him. Sparky recognized the voice and knew he was in trouble.

"Sparky?" God repeated.

"Yes," young Sparky replied.

"I've got a proposition. Do you see that solar system over there?"

Sparky gazed to where God had gestured and winced. It was Miss Saturn's neighborhood.

"Uh, yes, God? I see it."

"Do you remember it?"

Oh, boy, thought Sparky. *I'm in for it now.* "If this is about Miss Saturn..." Sparky started then stopped.

"I will take care of her," God said, "but I have a special project for you. That is..." God paused. "If you are willing to accept the responsibility."

"Responsibility?" Sparky asked.

"Extreme responsibility. In fact, Sparky, this is probably the one most important job in the entire universe."

Sparky quickly analyzed the situation. "Doing what?" He knew that was pushy, but still, he was young and could possibly get away with it.

"You won't be able to move," God stated. "For the rest of eternity you'll be stuck in one location. Are you still interested?"

Sparky was sure Miss Saturn was involved in this but couldn't figure out why the punishment was so harsh. Eternity! Unmoving! Then he remembered the horror stories he'd heard about Regis Comet.

"I'll do it," Sparky said.

"That's wonderful, my boy," God said. "I'm sure you'll do an excellent job. On the third planet from the sun, that blue one, my Son will be born tonight for all mankind. I want your light to guide all men who seek Him."

Sparky swelled with pride. That night he let loose all his pent up energy and shone doubly bright on the small manger in Bethlehem, knowing what a great honor had been bestowed upon him.

# # # # #

So there you have it, I told an old, solid theme -- the story of Christ's birth -- and found a new angle. I used the POV of the star to tell the tale. By doing so I was able to weave whimsy and fantasy together with a few realities. I didn't stoop to the age-worn tale of Santa, or a poor child on Christmas, or even a miracle.

After rewriting the story and sprucing it up some more I realized there were actually quite a few markets for it: children, religious, even science fiction or fantasy. I'd originally tossed the children's market aside thinking the story beyond their grasp. My mistake was attempting to be an editor and prejudging – in this case, under-estimating a child's grasp. This story would fit in Children's Highlights or Boys Life. It could even be in Guideposts, Fantasy Magazine, or any one of the many small, general magazines like The Ohioan or Country Today. Even a craft magazine will occasionally print a short-short like this.

When the season is upon you, the Muse will "slap you up along side the head" sometime during the period, letting you see a new angle. Write that story. Hone it. Then send it out in March to all the potential editors. Remember only an e-zine can accept a story in November for publication in December. The paper industry needs time—lots of time.

WEEK 11: Guest Writing Tip Entry...

Building A Successful Press Kit
by Mitchel Whitington

You're the proud parent of a shiny, new book. Published by yourself or a traditional house, it's been written, edited, printed, bound, and you're holding it in your hand. A job well-done, a job complete.

Or is it?

If you want to actually sell copies of the wonderful tome that you've written, then you're far from finished. A mighty task lies ahead: promotion! Without a strategic promotion effort, your book will simply sit on the bookshelves, or in boxes in your garage.

There are many facets to doing promotion, but one weapon that you will definitely need in your arsenal is a press kit. Whether you're using it to get reviews in newspapers, sending it ahead to bookstores where you'll be signing, or forwarding it to help publicize your speaking engagements, a press kit is definitely worth the small amount of time and money that it takes to produce.

If you've never seen one, a press kit is very simplistic in nature: a folder with pockets that contains information about your book. The type of information that is presented includes a synopsis of the book, an author bio, any clips, etc. The exact contents of any press kit vary with the author and book, but the items in the next section should be considered.

Ingredients of a Successful Press Kit

Book Synopsis: Long before a reviewer or interviewer gets your book in hand, someone is screening incoming queries for them. This person will be sorting through a heap of mail on their desk, and will only be able to give each item a few moments consideration. If your book comes clunking out of the envelope, it may be easier just to ignore it than to try to sift through the story and decide if it merits further consideration. A one-page synopsis, on the other hand, is easy to read and takes very little time -- something that will be greatly appreciated, and will be a mark in your favor when the book is being considered. Make it to the point and easy to read - after scanning it, they should know whether your book presents a money-making business opportunity, shows the reader how to grow award-winning roses, or contains the latest important medical information that is crucial to the average person.

Author Biography: A short biography one page at the most should be given to tell the reader exactly why you're interesting. If you are being considered for a radio interview, it doesn't matter if you got the attendance award in third grade, but if you've just completed a perilous canoe trip down an Alaskan river to research your new book, then you've just given the program a slant that they'd love to feature! Stick to the relevant facts, and add as much color as possible. Remember, you're selling yourself.

Clips: If your book has been reviewed in periodicals, be sure to include photocopies of the favorable articles. Quotes from radio and television interviews or reviews should also be included. Be prudent with what you include, however. Fifty photocopied reviews will turn off the screener, while two or three interesting ones will help to pique their interest.

Reviews/Quotes: Many books contain quotes from other authors on their jacket. Whether yours does or not, it's worth contacting some of your writer-friends for a sentence or two on your book. List several of these on a 'What They're Saying' page, and be sure to credit the author with their latest book. It helps them out, but it also lends credibility that a published author is commenting. These should be in the form:

'Riviting. A fantastic read. It taught me the hottest marketing techniques on the planet!' - Mitchel Whitington, The Book Constructor, and author of The Book Construction Kit.

Author Interview: Many interviewers will state that they don't use scripted questions, but this item is still a must. It gives the reader a flavor for the kind of responses that you might have during an interview. It provides background to use in an article, and it gives them questions to ask whether they admit it or not! Stay relevant and interesting, and keep the questions and answers to a single page.

Sample Chapters: Including a few sample chapters will give the reader a feel for your writing. You should especially consider this if you will not be sending a book in addition to your press kit. Be sure to select chapters that can stand-alone, are introductory, and that represent the book in the best possible light.

Unique Information: If there is anything unique about your book, be sure to incorporate it into your press kit. If you have a cookbook, for instance, you may want to include a recipe or two. If it's a life-success instructional, then give examples of people who have used your techniques.

Send-A-Book Cards: You can give the reader an opportunity to request the entire book by including a self-addressed, stamped postcard to return to you. If your book doesn't fit the venue that you've targeted, then the price of a promotional copy would have been saved by sacrificing a stamp.

Don't take these examples as a finite list for your press kit. Be creative, and include the items that make the most sense for your book.

A Case Study

When I was considering a press kit for my book, Uncle Bubba's Chicken Wing Fling, I wanted something that would reflect the light-hearted humor in the book. The story is set in the fictitious small Texas town of Cut Plug, so I drew on that fact and used the various organizations that the characters in the story belonged to.

For the folder I went to a local office supply store and found a plain (but attractive) deep purple folder. It contained an inside pocket on either side, and nothing more. To dress it up I used a printing package on my computer and made a small banner (about 6 inches by 3 inches) that read, 'Honorable Order of the Armadillo New Members' Manual,' complete with an armadillo clip-art. The Armadillo lodge is big in Cut Plug, so it was a good hook to use on the front. I printed it on glossy paper, cut it to size then attached it to the folder using adhesive spray from a local craft store.

For my bio, I printed a letterhead on blue paper that read, 'Cut Plug Police Department' with a badge logo and a few official-sounding phrases. Before listing my bio, I printed the words 'Police Report' across the top, and attached a wallet-sized photo to give some color to the page.

The Author Interview page was done on yellow paper with 'Cut Plug Garden Club' letterhead. I gave about five question/answers, including 'Just where is Cut Plug?' and 'What's next for Uncle Bubba?'

After soliciting several of my writer friends for blurbs about the book, I compiled a one-page issue of the 'Cut Plug Gazette' that contained all the kind words.

I worked enough information about the book in the Author Interview and Bio pages that I didn't feel the need for a synopsis. The loose sheets went into the left-hand pocket, and I put an armadillo graphic on one of the pockets for a little flair. When I send out the press kits, I write a personalized letter to the individual who will be reading it, and attach it to the front of the press kit with a small paper clip.

All the printing is done on my HP Inkjet printer using the highest quality print mode. I produce each kit myself, which gives me the flexibility to modify them for particular targets. Each press kit costs under three dollars to put together, and I've gotten wonderful comments on the package.

Good luck with yours, and remember, be creative. Whether or not your book makes it into a specific magazine, newspaper, or talk show may depend entirely on the press kit that the screener pulls out of the envelope!

© 2005 Mitchel Whitington

About the Author: Mitchel Whitington is an author and speaker - visit Mitchel's website at http://www.whitington.com/write/articles.htm.

A Timely Thought

My grandmother, who lived with us when I was a child, would spot a small rip in a shirt seam and immediately call me over to her while she grabbed a needle and thread. Quick as ever she'd whip the needle into the fabric and fix the offending seam. Then she'd say, 'A stitch in time, saves nine' to which I'd make the usual confused frown.

"Saves nine what, grandma?"

"Nine more stitches. Take care of it now with a quick stitch, or fix it with a major sewing repair later."

I was a young male and figured that phrase was obviously for girls only.

Well, I've matured and the many passing decades have been good to me. First, I've realized that 'girl stuff' is for the uninitiated. Other than giving birth, both sexes can do about anything they want, if they so desire. Therefore sewing is not for girls only.

Second. That phrase is very true, but for me, it doesn't relate to sewing. It's all about writing.

How many times have you thought of the perfect ending, great twist, or fantastic story only to lose it before you locked it on paper?

Perhaps you've not had to deal with it, but I've had that problem many times over the years and finally found a solution. It is a perfect solution, but not at my computer.

The solution actually came about in a very subtle manner. I was busy scribbling (pre-laptop days) down a short story I was working on during my several one hour train rides home from work. Suddenly a lightbulb turned on over my head and the problem I'd been trying to resolve in a book I had been working on was now blazingly apparent. I skipped to the back of the spiral notebook and jotted down the thought.

When I got home to my computer, I yanked the pad from my briefcase and dove into the book, correcting the bad plot I had labored over to the new one I'd thought about on the train.

On that same train, in the morning, I would fall asleep until it arrived at the station. During the transit, I would dream about different things, sometimes the chapter I was working on or future chapters. When

I awoke I'd rush to my office which was just outside the station. But unfortunately, by the time I'd get there, the dream was that, just a figment of my imagination.

Now I always carry a pen and notepad with me so I can write down any thoughts I have. When I'd awake from sleep on the train with a great idea, it was just a moment's delay and with said pen in hand, I was writing it down. Even if all I wrote were cryptic ideas of what I'd envisioned, the bottom line was: I had it on paper!

Of course, when you don't ride the train, but travel by personal car, some modification has to be made. Get a small hand-held tape recorder, but carry that notepad, nonetheless.

A wannabe will find every excuse why they can't write, the most common denominator being: not enough time. If you want to write, you'll find the time and I'll show you where you can glean some hidden minutes.

I've already discussed public transportation so I won't delve into that much further other than to say that my current forty-five minute bus ride has allowed me time to write quite a few short stories. Plus, sometimes you'll get lucky and have a newly self-proclaimed editor sitting next to you, reading over your shoulder and correcting or suggesting.

I'm sure the eyebrows went up when I said personal car. I know you're driving, but do you really need to listen to the radio? If you're headed for a traffic jam, more than likely all other routes are going to be just as congested. So, when given lemons, make lemonade. Use a handheld tape recorder and talk away. You can always type it in later and more than likely enhance what you noted. The major item here is: you have the basics down. At least when you're sitting at the keyboard, you can be typing in what you already have, not thinking about what you're going to do. To attempt this in a car-pool can be difficult, at best, either as the driver or passenger.

I was in a major traffic snarl for 1-1/2 hours. Did I fume and get upset? Yeah, a little, but I also got some major writing completed. I used my notepad and had the radio going. An occasional look over my dash told me that traffic wasn't moving, yet.

Lunch time. That's a given. Grab a quick meal and drink; head to the park or nearby bench and write. Do you really need to sit with the gang and gossip every day? Even sitting at your desk, if allowed, to eat your meal and work is getting some writing done. Remember, lunch is YOUR time, use it.

Waiting rooms. I've done my stint in waiting rooms. Sure, at times it will appear callous to be sitting there typing away on a laptop or writing in a notepad. Writers are people of experience. Use the emotion of the moment and write. It will move you farther along toward your goal instead of sitting there reading old magazines or watching cartoons on the television. Waiting rooms are for waiting; be it another fifteen minutes until the doctor sees you or three hours awaiting the outcome of the surgery. It is waiting time, not wasting time.

A stitch in time saves nine. Actually, it means something totally different from what my grandmother taught me. A note in time saves nine re-writes trying to remember that lone lost moment.

Do I actually save time? Sure. This article was conceived, written, and first-pass edited on bus rides, during which, one time, I had the pleasure to endure a traffic snarl to delay my trip home by almost forty-five minutes. This same article was typed in during lunch, with the final edits performed at home.

So, my question is -- Are you wannabe filled with lame excuses?

Poetry Fun

Poetry usually gets a bad rap. It's boring, tedious, dull, dreaded, and downright yucky. Some would rather shove bamboo splints under their nails, receive a lobotomy, or slash their wrists than be subjected to poetry. Nonetheless, poetry can be fun. How, you ask? Simple. Take the following mathematical poem written by Jon Saxton, an author of math textbooks.

$$((12 + 144 + 20 + (3 * 4^{(1/2)})) / 7) + (5 * 11) = 9^2 + 0$$

Yes, it IS a poem. If read properly, it will rhyme AND be mathematically correct.

For those who can't figure it out...the answer will be found at the bottom of this article. I don't think I'd dare force you to wait until the next issue. I'll give you a hint, 12 is read as "a dozen" and my apologies if you were actually attempting to figure it out.

> Jack and Jill went up the hill
> Each had a quarter
> Jill came down with fifty cents
> Did they go up for water?

You say the above poems didn't bring a smile to your face? What if I were to mention limericks? See? A secret smile blossomed as you remembered some risqué ditty. I won't subject you to limericks... this time!

During my English and Lit classes, poetry was often expounded upon by the instructor. And I dreaded it! I attempted the "deep" style, but found that my spirit was too light to be bogged down in such. Speaking with others, I've come to discover that I'm not the only person who found a lighter side. Poetry can be light-hearted and still have a meaning. Samantha Adley, a screenwriter who is also a serious poet, submitted the following as a class assignment.

SHADOW

> Found a place called If Only,
> Right next to Instead,
> Tried to grab its shadow,
> But Shadow quickly fled.
> Seemed so silly simple,

But silly simple clear
That Shadow left a message,
"Fear the lack of Fear."
Shadow left me holding pieces
Of Rainbow's brilliant hues,
Ate'em up like candy,
Ate up Shadow, too.
Sing a song of six-pence,
Pocket full of dread,
Traced forgotten footprints
Deep inside my head.
Old now is Used to Be,
And Later Never Was,
Comes a crowd of Wonder Whys,
Looking for Because.
"Quickly," said Forever,
"Later becomes Soon,"
Laughter winks her traitorous eye
And pricks a child's balloon.
'Twixt pages of an unbook,
In fragmented hues,
Bleeds a shattered butterfly
In Red and Pain and Blue.
In the streets of Wish I Had,
The hawker hawks his wares,
"Too soon old; too late smart,
Buy your clichés here."
Left the place called If Only,
Left Instead behind,
Turned Outside Inside,
Found Shadow in my mind.

Samantha Adley © 2000

Needless to say, her instructor was not amused. He accused her of taking light on poetry and mocking it. Like a good rebel, she took exception and submitted a similar poem for her next assignment.

Poetry can place us in front of a mirror, for there is the real humor. Man is the only creature on earth who can laugh, ridicule, and make fun of itself. Poetry can also do this. The following is a great example by that great unknown, Anonymous, which makes us laugh at ourselves by showing us, us!

'Twas an evening in November,
And I very well remember,
I was walking down the street in drunken pride.
But my knees went all a'flutter,
and I landed in the gutter,
and a pig walked up and lay down by my side.
Now I lie there in the gutter,
Thinking thoughts I dare not utter,
When a colleen, passing by, did softly say:
"You can tell a man who boozes,
by the company he chooses".
And at that, the pig got up and walked away!

Anonymous

I hope that I've shown you that poetry can be fun. There are many examples if you but give yourself a chance to look. Oh, before I forget. Here's the answer to the mathematical poem from above. Enjoy.

The Poem

$$((12 + 144 + 20 + (3 * 4^{(1/2)})) / 7) + (5 * 11) = 9^2 + 0$$

A dozen, a gross and a score,
plus three times the square root of four,
divided by seven,
plus five times eleven,
equals nine squared and not a bit more.

As I hit the highway in search of more tips, I leave you with these departing words from a master, Ogden Nash, in his 1933 "Happy Days" Song of the Road.

I think that I shall never see
A billboard as lovely as a tree
Perhaps, unless the billboards fall
I'll never see a tree at all.

Ogden Nash

WEEK 14:

Youthful Poetry

Let's play the word association game. I'll give you two words, and you find the link.

Poetry ~ Kids

Hmm. I'd be willing to bet you had to think hard on that one, or else a nursery, jump/skip rope, or cliché rhyme came to mind. Most adults don't associate poetry composition and adolescence together. But think, when did you first hear a poem? Answer: Infant. When did you learn about poetry? Answer: Elementary school. When did you compose your first poem? Answer: Probably before age ten.

My point? Poetry is not only for adults, nor only by adults.

A crystal
snowflake
falls down
on the
freezing
white
floor
of January.

© Martha Bregin, 1999 All Rights Reserved

Fantastic imagery in only twelve words, the number of months in a year. This poem was written by Martha Bregin, a second-grader from Pine Knob Elementary School in Independence Township near Detroit, MI. Yes, you read correctly. Martha was only eight-years-old back in 1999. She was in competition with thousands of other schoolchildren from kindergarten through twelfth grade. Miss Bregin won the kindergarten through second-grade category of the River of Words International Poetry and Art Contest that is sponsored by International Rivers Network. IRN (www.irn.org) is a non-profit organization located in California dedicated to preserving the world's rivers. I'll also note that Martha Bregin accepted her award and performed a public reading at the Library of Congress in Washington, DC. Impressive start for an eight-year-old lass. Her poem and those of the other category winners will be soon available in a book.

Do you have a son? A daughter? Talk with them. I was taken off-guard by my own son when I was discussing this article. Seems I have a "closet" poet in the family. He retrieved his little beat-up binder pad of poetry he has used to compose poems over the years and started reciting. Yes, years! My son was nineteen and amazed me back in 1999 and still does to this day. Perhaps "closet" was a poor choice in words. I discovered during our conversation he usually composes his poetry while in bed in the morning; as he said "with the sunlight coming through the window, it's really neat. It makes you think." So here are a couple of poems my son allowed me to use.

Before the Sun Comes Around

Early in the morning
Before the sun comes
The wind blows lightly
And morning birds sing songs.
If I had to describe Heaven,
This is what it would be.
Some would say angels and clouds
But as for me,
It's when it's still dim
With just a little sound.
That magic moment
Before the sun comes around.

© Rob Nailor, 1996 All Rights Reserved

Time

Time goes by oh so fast
The only thing we can do
Is look back on memories
Shared with family and friends
In hopes that those relationships
Will never end.
So make your life a joyous ride
Cause time goes by
In the blink of an eye.

© Rob Nailor, 1997 All Rights Reserved

So, the next time you see a small child making a face, learning to ride a bike, or playing on the teeter-totter, just remember you may be seeing the makings of a future great poet of the world.

?

The Top 10 Things You Must Know About Radio Interviews
by Mitchel Whitington

Radio interviews can be one of the most powerful avenues of publicity that you'll find - yet so many people live in dread of getting on live radio. Since 1999, I've done hundreds of them, and they're fairly easy now. They didn't start out that way, though... I was terrified!

There are a few simple points that can help anyone become a radio pro...

1. Landing interviews isn't as mysterious as you might think. Radio show producers have the job of booking interesting guests on the program. Now that certainly doesn't mean you can automatically get on their program just by asking, but present yourself in an interesting way you certainly stand a chance. Two of the best ways

2. If talking to a large group of people scares you, forget the audience! You know this if you've done radio before, but the vast majority of all interviews occur in the privacy of your home or office. You'll pre-arrange a time with the station, they'll call you, and it will be almost exactly like you're simply talking to someone on the phone. So many people get completely freaked out by the idea that thousands and thousands of people might be listening to the interview - but get a correct mindset to control this fear! Pretend that you're simply talking to a friend, or that there are only a handful of people out there. Once you get into the interview, and with a little experience behind you, it's easy to adopt that frame of mind... you're just talking to a friend on the phone.

3. Try to work in regional information. Although it's not always the case, you'll usually have at least twenty-four hours to prepare. If there's some way that you can relate your book or interview topic to their region, chances are you'll get more airtime. Use the Internet to look up statistics or information pertaining to your discussion, and before the interview, work out a plan for weaving it into the conversation.

4. Always be ready to go at a moment's notice. Once you've sent press kits and query letters to radio stations, they will keep the information in their files. One of the reasons for this is that if they need a last-minute guest, they'll have a large selection of guests at their fingertips. If this happens, though, you might get a last minute call saying, "Can you be on the air in 10 minutes?" If that happens, there can only be

one answer: YES! If you work from notes, always have them in a file that you can access immediately. Personally, I don't; I just sit and mentally go over previous interviews, getting into the right mindset to get started right away. Whatever the case is with you, just be ready to be called for a last-minute performance.

5. Get the details. When the producer of a radio show calls you to set up the interview, there are a few things that you have to write down. The first is the time... but just as important, the time zone. I've had the phone ring and someone say, "Okay, you're on in 5... 4... 3..." I'd say, "Wait! You said 9 AM!" The voice answered, "It is 9 AM - here on the east coast!" Learn how to calculate time zones if you don't already know. Also, be sure to ask how they found out about you. That will let you know which of your promotional avenues are working.

6. Find out who'll you'll be talking to. One more thing to ask during the set-up phone call. You'll also need to write down the exact names of the persons you'll be speaking to in the interview - although I've never had this happen, I have friends who spent an entire interview calling DeeJay James by the name "Johnny". Not a good thing. Find out who everyone on the show is, and how they want to be addressed.

7. Send a free book to give away on the air. You will want to mention this during the set-up phone call as well, if there's enough time before the interview to get a book to them. Radio stations love to give things away to listeners, so if they can tie in a book giveaway with your interview, it can actually add time to your segment. I've used this technique many times, and it works well.

8. Mention your book/website repeatedly. It is so easy to get lost in talking about the facts of an interview, and forget to mention your book name and/or website. If you over-mention them, it's going to turn off the interviewer and the audience, so try to strike a happy medium between not saying it at all, and bombarding the audience with it. My rule of thumb is that: if you think that you're saying it too much, you probably are. If you think that you're not saying it enough, you probably aren't.

9. Be prepared for a call to go terribly wrong. No one wants this to happen, but it does. One of my best writer-friends in the world got a call to be on the "Snake and The Bruiser Show" in New York. When she started the interview, one DeeJay was serious and sincere, while the other asked the most horrid, irreverent questions. As it turned out,

"Snake and The Bruiser" were shills from the Howard Stern show, and the entire thing was a terrible setup. While that extreme example probably won't happen to you, be prepared for some "shock jock" to turn on you at a moment's notice. Their mission is to offend you enough to get you to hang up the phone, which to be honest, you'll probably end up doing. Hang on as long as you can, answering offensive questions with "bypass answers" like, "Well, I don't know about that, but at mywebsite.com you can certainly find out about my book." Some people say that there's no such thing as bad publicity, so just hang on while you can, and get your name/website out there when you can.

10. After the interview, send a thank-you email. Some folks swear that it should be a tangible, paper letter, but not me. We live in an electronic world, and producers keep electronic files. Send them an email, and they'll file it in their "great guest" mailbox (or wherever they keep their good information). Also, radio folks also have on-line industry bulletin boards where they list good guests, and sending a heart-felt "thank you" can help them remember to post your name there.

© 2005 Mitchel Whitington

About the Author: Mitchel Whitington is an author and speaker - visit Mitchel's website at http://www.whitington.com/write/articles.htm.

Oh Horrors! Children's Writing

When was the first time you got scared? Can't remember back that far? Writing horror for children is a fine art that can be easily mastered by following simple guidelines.

Ray Bradbury once said we should remember our childhood vulnerability as we approach our writing. Remember the monster under your bed? How about the closet? Or even that mean bully or adult? Don't forget the vacation, the campout, or even (gasp!) the basement!

Monster: To scare you, the monster must have some human traits but not necessarily be human. Don't forget Frankenstein had a soft side, a childlike quality. That was the redeeming social grace which endeared him to us, yet all the while his raging anger was to be feared. Still, your monster need not be human. Stephen King used a dog, Amityville was a house and Bradbury used a town with a circus.

Graphic Violence: When dealing with children, the amount of violence must never be graphic. You can cut off someone's head, but you don't need to go into the gory details of the act. Our imagination will supply the proper amount of gory graphics for a violent scene to scare us, sometimes too much.

Anticipation: Without that there is no story. We read and all the while have created our little anticipated ideas of where the line is going. A good writer will lead you down the rosy path to scare the tarnations out of you from time to time.

Pacing: Notice I said 'from time to time' in the previous paragraph. You can't have high terror the whole time. You must pace your story, make it a roller-coaster ride of highs and lows. But remember, all during this time, there must be a niggling in the back of the mind. The reader has to be at the edge of the chair hoping and waiting for the next big scare.

Atmosphere: Your story should have a dark side. Most horror stories don't take place on a beautiful, sunlight day with birds and bees and white fluffy clouds. You can start out that way, but you want your reader to become scared of the shadows. Shadows are the writer's friend and the reader's concern. Think about this: Even on a bright day, if someone jumps out of the bushes and scares you... that person came from the shadows of the bushes; a location you couldn't see beforehand. This is the writer's advantage.

Your characters in the story are the actual ingredient some writers skim over in favor of the monster. Don't.

Hero (or Heroine): This is the person the monster has singled out. The monster needs to make our hero feel vulnerable and alone. Usually the creature will zero in on the one weakness or fear our hero has and then use it to the creature's advantage. The depth of your hero's character is the crux of your story.

Friends: Not all your hero's friends should buy into the monster theory. By doing this there is more room for story advancement as the creature attacks those who don't or won't believe. Even when the monster is in the room, there should be those who don't believe or want to believe.

Adults: This is children writing specific. Adults are usually the enemy of children and therefore can't be trusted. Of course, there's a rule broken every minute. You'll have one adult who will believe -- if not help evolve the monster -- and could be crucial at the proper moment. This is the writer's call. Sometimes adults aren't involved in the story at all or play superfluous parts.

Non-believers: You just have to have the nay-sayers; what more can be said? Not everyone is going to be encouraging and approving of what is happening.

Plot: Your hero, no matter how grave the situation, must have an out; a reasonable, logical out. If you fluff your hero's escape, you'll lose your reader. I was once told by a writing friend of fantasy that when you put a wizard into battle, you'd better have a way out other than zapping him away. A proper wizard would never go into battle with the idea of zapping away when things got tough. This is true for your hero and monster. If things get tough, have an out for them to continue the story line; otherwise, kill the character at that moment.

Sex: Excuse me, you're writing for children. There is NO sex. Jeesh! Depending on the age, maybe a little peck of a kiss or perhaps some hand-holding, but that's the extent of sex for a children's book.

So there you have it. Shadows, lots of shadows, a good friend or two, a friendly monster of some sort who just happens to know your one major fear or fault, and a lot of people who don't believe in you, but you believe in yourself and your ability.

If you need a bit more help, R. L. Stein has a book or two out the kids seem to enjoy. Read them for a bit more insight.

WEEK 17:

Use Climax in Writing

First, this is not about sex.

The use of climax in fictional writing is how all writers make their work exciting and action-packed. In order for climax to be effective, it must be both relevant to the story and impact the story's protagonist, antagonist or key characters. Climax can be a little complicated to work into a story without it being obvious or awkward.

1) <u>Involve important characters</u>. The climax of the story is the point at which the conflict reaches a boiling point, the mystery gets solved or a life-changing event occurs. Since it will involve one or more of the major plots of the story, it makes sense that one or more of the main characters will be involved as well.

2) <u>Set the climax in an appropriate setting</u>. The setting of the climax goes a long way towards making it more exciting, dangerous or meaningful. Set your climax next to the grave of a murder victim, in a dark forest or in a warehouse that has been set ablaze. A climax that takes place in one of these locations will obviously be more effective than one set in a grocery store or someone's garage.

3) <u>Create the unexpected</u>. You will want your climax to ultimately be one that none of your readers see coming, the kind that will cause them to gasp out loud and keep them reading until the end. So don't be afraid to think outside the box for your climactic event and throw a few curveballs into the plot. Have the murder suspect save the day, one of your characters turn out to be undiscovered royalty or reveal the love affair between your story's protagonist and antagonist. Plot twists like these, right as the climax action of the story is taking place will make your story unforgettable.

4) <u>Work the climax into the story reasonably</u>. The action of your climax must not be discounted by the improbability of it occurring. Your climax should be exciting and unexpected, but it still needs to be feasibly possible. You can work the climax in seamlessly and still keep it exciting by using false conclusion, in which your protagonist intends to do one thing and is then forced or compelled to do another, the latter being your climax action. You can also change the setting of the scene abruptly so that the reader never sees the climax coming. If your characters are in the car taking a leisurely drive one moment and are careening over a cliff

while one admits to killing the other's brother, your reader will be caught by surprise at the urgency and unexpectedness of the situation and also by the revelation of the characters. Thus, you have created life-changing events that could really happen that will change the end of the book completely.

Ten Points on Plotting

1. <u>Nothing should happen at random</u>. Every element in a story should have significance, whether for verisimilitude, symbolism, or the intended climax. Names, places, actions and events should all be purposeful. To test the significance of an element, ask: Why this place and not another? Why this name and not another? Why this action, this speech, and not others--or none at all? The answers should be: To persuade the reader of the story's plausibility; to convey a message about the theme of the story; to prepare the reader for the climax so that it seems both plausible and in keeping with the theme.

2. <u>Plot stems from character under adversity</u>. A mild-mannered person cannot achieve his goals by an out-of-character action like a violent assault, unless we have prepared the reader for it by revealing a glimpse of some suppressed aspect of his personality that can be plausibly released by stress. And the stress itself must also be plausible, given the circumstances of the story.

3. <u>Each character has an urgent personal agenda</u>. Too much is at stake to abandon that agenda without good reason. We may not share the character's urgency, but we should be able to see why he cares so much about what he's doing. A character who acts without real motivation is by definition melodramatic, doing outrageous things for the sake of the thrill it gives the reader--not because it makes sense for the character to do so.

4. <u>The plot of a story is the synthesis of the plots of its individual characters</u>. Each character has a personal agenda, modified by conflict or concordance with the agendas of others. The villain doesn't get everything his way, any more than the hero does; each keeps thwarting the other, who must then improvise under pressure. If the hero is moving northwest, and the villain is moving northeast, the plot carries them both more or less due north--at least until one or the other gains some advantage.

5. <u>The plot "begins" long before the story</u>. The story itself should begin at the latest possible moment before the climax, at a point when events take a decisive and irreversible turn. We may learn later, through flashbacks, exposition, or inference, about events occurring before the beginning of the story.

6. <u>Foreshadow all important elements</u>. The first part of a story is a kind of prophecy; the second part fulfills the prophecy. Any important character, location, object should be foreshadowed early in the story. The deus ex machina is unacceptable; you can't pull a rabbit out of your hat to rescue your hero. But you can't telegraph your punch either--your readers don't want to see what's coming, especially if your characters seem too dumb to see it. The trick is to put the plot element into your story without making the reader excessively aware of its importance. Chance and coincidence, in particular, require careful preparation if they are going to influence the plot.

7. <u>Keep in mind the kind of story you're telling</u>. Any story is about the relationship of an individual to society. A comic story describes an isolated individual achieving social integration either by being accepted into an existing society or by forming his own. This integration is often symbolized by a wedding or feast. A tragic story describes an integrated individual who becomes isolated; death is simply a symbol of this isolation. The plot should keep us in some degree of suspense about what kind of story we're reading. Even if we know it's a comedy, the precise nature of the comic climax should come as a surprise. If we know the hero is doomed, his downfall should stem from a factor we know about but have not given sufficient weight to.

8. <u>Ironic plots subvert their surface meanings</u>. Here, an ordinarily desirable goal appears very unattractive to us: the hero marries, but chooses the wrong girl and turns his story into a tragedy. Or the hero may die, but gains some improvement in social acceptance as a result--by becoming a martyr or social savior, for example.

9. <u>The hero must eventually take charge of events</u>. In any plot the hero is passive for a time, reacting to events. At some point he must try to take charge. This is the counter thrust, when the story goes into high gear. In some cases we may have a series of thrusts and counter thrusts; in the opening stages of the plot, the counter thrust helps define the hero's character and puts him in position for more serious conflicts (and counter thrusts) later in the story. You could even say that every scene presents the hero with a problem; his response is his counter thrust. In the larger structure of the plot, the counter thrust often comes after the hero's original plan of action has failed; he has learned some hard lessons and now he will apply them as he approaches the climax of the story.

10. <u>Plot dramatizes character</u>. If all literature is the story of the quest for identity, then plot is the roadmap of that quest. Every event,

every response, should reveal (to us if not to them) some aspect of the characters' identities. Plot elements dramatize characters' identities by providing opportunities to be brave or cowardly, stupid or brilliant, generous or mean. These opportunities come in the form of severe stress, appropriate to the kind of story you're telling. A plot element used for its own sake--a fistfight, a sexual encounter, an ominous warning--is a needless burden to the story if it does not illuminate the characters involved. Conversely, the reader will not believe any character trait that you have not dramatized through a plot device.

A Couple of Horror Secrets

I tend to write what some people call 'soft horror' or 'twisted' type stories. No, I do not write a lot of blood, guts and gore — or as I call it: *bg&g*. Of course, I'm not saying that bg&g is a bad thing but I tend to lean more toward the psychological type horror. Yes, I love to play with your mind... take it out, massage it, squeeze it and then give it a good twist before putting it back into the cavity.

So how can you write a horror story that scares the crap out of your reader and not have bg&g?

1) <u>Place your creature in a strange place or distant location</u>. Huh? Strange place? Do you expect to find a vampire stalking the halls of a hospital or prison? Get them out of those drafty castles and dank dungeons. Place some in a dilapidated plantation in a deep, vibrant Southern bayou... and make them young children. Do your zombies wander the streets of the town or do they attack out of the piles of trash at a landfill? Even glowing demon eyes at the bottom of the basement stairs can send chills coursing up and down your readers' spines.

2) <u>Expand on the dark human nature</u>. Not all monsters have to be supernatural... the ol' human body is just fine. The evil lurking deep inside the psyche of a demented person can be your 'muse' for the next story - think "Hannibal" for an idea. Yes, I'm talking about cannibalism and other very taboo topics which respectable society now frowns upon. A nice, elderly couple befriending a run-away girl still need to eat... or is it the other way around?

3) <u>Abuse is a no-no</u>. Child abuse is even a bigger no-no. Attempt to avoid any situation where a child is involved. I'm not saying you can't have children as victims but it needs to be addressed properly. Let the reader's imagination fill in the blanks. I think the movie was "Warlock" and he wanted to make a candle and needed untainted human tallow when he stumbled upon a child who was unbaptized. The next scene showed him with the candle. I still get chills when I think of that scene.

4) <u>Where to get ideas</u>? Read your local newspaper and when a certain aspect grabs you in a story, write the concept down. Let your imagination run rampant when doing this. Also check out news articles on the internet. AND the bestest ever place to get an idea -- your nightly dreams. Keep that notebook beside your bed and when a nightmare

awakes you, write it down. Trust me, by morning that terrifying experience will have mellowed and might even be just a dissipated thought you will struggle to remember for days and fail in this goal.

Good psychological horror is the ability to take the ordinary and make it extraordinary. In other words, that cup of coffee sitting in front of you, is it really coffee or some strange creature about to consume you from the inside out, or is it really Joe?

Author Websites

The number one necessity for an author in today's publishing market is a website. Oftentimes, a reader will finish a book and immediately search for the author online, looking for their website to see what else they have written and what they are working on. Your webpage can be simple or complex, it all depends on your own ability at webpage programming, the time you can commit, or the amount of money you are able to pay someone else to make a page for you.

The most important information to have on your site is your works. The website is about selling your books to readers and everything you write should be included. You should also include a bio, probably one that is more detailed than the bio you use for books. You also want to have a blog, which we will discuss later, and ways for people to contact you. Oftentimes if you have a website, you can set up an email through that website. If not, create a new email address through any of the regular free email providers you will use only for keeping in touch with your fans. You will also want to link your webpage to your Twitter, Goodreads and Facebook accounts. One thing you should be sure to do, is have a link from your works to whatever outlets are selling them, so that if a person likes your blurb for your book, they click the link and go to Amazon or the publisher's site so they can buy the book.

Most authors include all this information on their pages, but there is one more item which should be included on your website: a 'work-in-progress' page. If your readers know you are working on something, and you give occasional updates on the progress, they will come back to your page to get more details. If you include a release schedule for your books since they have been watching the progress, they will be waiting for that day and will buy your book.

The first thing you need to do to set up a website is find a webhost. There are many out there at a variety of prices. May I suggest HostGator.com, iPage.com, GoDaddy.com, Dreamhost.com or bluehost.com? There are many out there, and a search using your favorite web search engine and entering "webhost providers" will give you many possibilities to review. Just be sure to verify what you are getting – some providers place web ads on your pages which can cheapen your appearance.

Next you need to build your website. You can do this with simple graphics, including your book covers, or if you are talented at graphic design, know someone who is, or are willing to pay the price for a professional, you can fill your page with outstanding graphics, the choice is yours. Simple is the way to go unless you have an artistic eye. Remember, flashy graphics can catch a person's interest, but the most important thing on the page is the content. Three things to avoid like the plague – colorful flashing text, fancy cursors and uncontrollable music or sounds.

As for the actual building of said site, there are many different options. You can find website builders who require you to know how to use code, or ones who simply allow you to place what you want, where you want it. A quick search of the internet will show you software which allows you to create web pages; some may be free, some reasonable, some expensive.

Now, about that blog. Any writer worth their salt must have a blog where they allow the readers to get to know them. Yes, your website is one way, but a blog can be more personal or even professional. I have a blog where I "ramble on" about almost anything, usually writing and I also do a weekly writing tip which is separate from the blog.

John Locke suggests that a blog be 'to the point' for the reader. He claims to only update his blog every six to eight weeks, if that often. My friend does a daily blog which I find to a very ambitious aspiration. I do my blog and writing tip weekly and that takes quite a bit of time. Once you begin to gain followers, you must continue to produce the blog. Maybe you can skip one week but if you allow yourself to skip once, you'll allow yourself to skip twice and then the blog will become old and stale. If I visit a person's blog and it hasn't changed over a period of time, I have to figure out if the person has died, given it up, or just doesn't have anything to say. Of course, while I'm attempting to decipher the lack of updates, I often decide to not bother coming back.

This also holds true for many websites. If they become static and never seem to change, then why should I spend my time looking to see if it has been updated? As a visitor to a blog and/or a website, why waste my time? I have better things to do.

Get your website or blog up and running. Keep it alive and changing. Good luck.

Freelance: How To Sell Almost Everything You Write

I was speaking with an acquaintance at a writing seminar and from out of nowhere, he said, "I write cheesy material." Now I wasn't exactly sure how to respond, so rather than let the conversation die, I decided the proper thing to do was inquire. So I asked, "How cheesy?" Through the conversation I discovered he had written many articles about a topic very dear to him: cheese.

Yes, reader, there is at least one magazine available for almost every type of devotee's desire; be it cheese, basset hounds, model planes, carving, wines, running, even candle stick making.

Where would you sell cheese articles? Many cooking magazines are available, even a wine magazine would be interested in an esoteric article about the use and history of goat cheese. One should also consider the local "farm" magazines such as Dairy Today or Ohio Farmer. Don't forget regional and state magazines like Sunset or Montana Magazine.

Need a bit more help? How about trade magazines? If you'd like a nicely listed grouping of different trades, check out: http://www.magazines.com/ and of course, Writer's Market is a viable resource, too. Some categories are limited, but others, such as computers, have many possibilities, breaking down into sub-categories like networks, operating systems, computer types, and software.

Freelancing is easiest when you write about what you know. It's a worn and haggard cliché, but the truth is there. When you write what you know, you're writing from the heart and it reflects in the final product and tends to make the sale just a little easier. Actually, the fastest and easiest money is there when you already know the subject and don't need to invest a lot of time researching. Of course, research is always a good thing, especially if you want to give your article that extra special punch.

Remember, specialty magazine readerships are in the lower numbers, unlike Time or Newsweek, and as such, probably don't have a large staff to create the articles they publish. Hence, freelancing will fill their needs and your coffers.

If you love it, you can write it. If you write it, they will buy it.

Dialogue and Detail

I was asked, as a reader, which do I prefer - dialogue or narrative?

That was a hard question. Narrative is great because you just read along and the author explains it all as he goes—sort of like the narrator for all those wonderful National Geographic films about whales, penguins, jungles and such. The image is projected into your mind's eye and as you read, it is like a movie.

But the reality is simple. Dialogue is a part of your character. Unless they are mute, your characters have to communicate—so, in reality, if they were mute, they'd still communicate through signs and actions.

As a reader, any writer who can give convincing dialogue without all the daily mundane sounds "How are you?" can make the story move along very nicely. When I write my first pass, I basically tell the story using dialogue.

My friend, a beta-reader for my rough first passes, brought it to my attention through a very unique description. He said: *Reading your stories is like listening to a stage production prior to dress rehearsal and the addition of props. It is interesting but I only get to hear about the action. I want to see the action, know the colors and feel the wind on my face.*

I have found narrative interesting but sometimes I feel the characters are lacking due to very little conversation skills on their behalf.

In literal narrative, you'd read *The young deputy returned to the office and told the sheriff he'd spoken with Cooter and learned about Mr. Wilson's involvement.*

While with dialogue you'd get something like *The sheriff wanted more details. Deputy Wade Hall pulled up to the dilapidated house. An old man sat rocking in his chair on the porch. "So, Cooter, did you see that young girl or not?" The young deputy eyed the old man suspiciously. "If'n y'all done come earlier—" Cooter leaned over, spit and hit the tin-can spittoon with dead-on accuracy. "You'd see'd her with ol' man Wilson from the dime-store." Cooter pointed at the kudzu entwined trees beyond the fence. "The two of dem were wandering back in dem woods. Theys done left."* The deputy nodded and headed back to the car to let the sheriff know about Wilson's sudden involvement.

By using dialogue you were able to make Cooter a character and give some flavor of the locale - obviously in the South since kudzu hasn't quite made it to the North... yet.

So, personally, I love dialogue and do most of my first-pass writing as dialogue then go back and add the ambiance of descriptions, personalities, etc. In other words — I create dress rehearsal. You can do the same — add dialogue to your story which will help describe what/where/why while at the same time, move the story along.

⁇

Instant Einstein

When you write a story, usually you do a little research. Okay, maybe you do an immense amount of research. I know I do.

Why do you do this?

The answer is simple. Authenticity. If you were to just make up stuff as you wrote, the story could ring shallow. In fact, your readers will quickly realize that you are Blue Skying aka BS-ing them. Let me give you some examples of what I did to become knowledgeable of my subject matter.

In my novel, "2012: Timeline Apocalypse," I was out of my element to some extent. I'd been through the Panama Canal and had spent a week in Acapulco with a couple of day trips to see ruins. I had 'some' background to work with but, still, I wanted my story to ring with a little more reality than what I could remember of my trip back in the late 1960s. So I started to research.

Originally my story was going to take place in Chichen Itza but I quickly realized that it was extremely too commercial for what I wanted to happen. I stumbled on Palenque and the great Mayan chief, Pacal. A little more research gave me his tomb which added to my story. Suddenly the story took on better depth and the Temple of Inscriptions came alive for me with other hidden possibilities. I now had historical data, a real location and my wild imagination.

Of course, having the ruins located a short distance from the city help add some ambiance. It allowed my character to embrace the locale, the freedom, the people and the way of life.

Some more research gave me legends, myths and local religion. I added Mayan gods and used some of the ancient Mayan words to create names. I was consumed by what I was learning.

For my novel "Three Steps: The Journeys of Ayrold" I was intrigued by Ireland, home of my grandfather. Again, I started research and learned about Celtic magic, charms, potions and myths. With this in-depth studying, my story evolved from a lame tale of a man searching for his past to a story of a man learning who he is, who he was and who he wants to be. I used my old tromping grounds where I grew up during high school for the beginning of the story but I've never been to Ireland. I needed to rely on the internet and local library to give me information. (*Let me interject a note here -- don't rely on the internet as the sole resource, not everything on the internet is true!*)

To make my leprechaun characters unique -- I got my idea from a sign I saw in a town I was passing through on my trip from Washington, DC back to NW Ohio. So, yes, the story has many true facts. One tidbit, I actually went to the Sheraton hotel on Connecticut Ave and rode the elevator to the 3rd floor and reviewed it. Things may have changed since then (1996) but still, at the time, it was an accurate description. Oh, by the way, the Mexican restaurant really did have some of the best tasting tacos at very reasonable prices! The restaurant with its bistro patio was a great place to have lunch.

To sum it up, I became an instant Einstein, a fount of knowledge for my novels. Some of what I learned has stuck with me but much of it has dissipated into the nether realms. Still, for a brief moment in life, I was an Einstein.

WEEK 24:

Whose Who's Whose?

The answer is simple – It's its.

That was mean and I apologize. For many readers and even more writers, knowing when to use "whose" vs "who's" is really quite simple by remembering a silly rule exception.

As youth, we are taught about possessives. This is Bob's document. That is Sally's cat. The rule is: Use an "apostrophe s" to indicate ownership. So obviously "who's" would be correct – WRONG!

Remember the old adage – *There is an exception to every rule?*

So it is with this.

As we learned to read we were introduced to 'cannot' and 'he is' plus others. To make the words easier, we were taught about contractions; eliminate a couple of letters and stick in an apostrophe. Therefore, phrases like "cannot" becomes "can't" and "he is" becomes "he's."

Want to play with "it's" and "its" for a little while? One is a contraction, another is possessive.

Did I mention something about an adage and exceptions to the rule?

Right. "Its" is possessive and "it's" is the contraction. So much for the possession rule.

Rule 1: "apostrophe s" is used to denote ownership.

Except for "who's" and "it's" – they become "whose" and "its."

Rule 2: use an apostrophe to concatenate two words.

So "it is" and "who is" becomes "it's" and "who's."

Therefore "who's" is a contraction for "who is" or "who has" and "it's" is a contraction for "it is" which is contradictory to the rules of possession.

So, to make things easier to understand, use the following guidelines for these words...

1. If you can say "who is" or "who has" – then use "who's" in the sentence.

2. If you can say "it is" – then use "it's" in the sentence.

3. Otherwise, use "whose" or "its" in the sentence.

Really? You didn't understand that? Try the following sentences--

-

(Who's/Whose) car is that in the driveway? You wouldn't say "who is" or "who has" so obviously "Whose" is the correct choice.

(It's/Its) the correct way to do things. You would say "it is" so therefore "it's" is the proper choice.

What is (it's/its) priority? Obviously "it is" doesn't fit, so "its" is correct.

(Who's/Whose) watching the baby? With this sentence, "who is" is correct, so "Who's" is the answer.

I hope the above has helped to clarify where to use "whose," "who's," "its," and "it's." After all, think about it this way – It's whose job to make it right? Yours!

Point of View aka POV

Exactly what is POV? To begin, it is not the easiest thing to describe but I will attempt something feeble.

I would call POV the perspective view the reader of a story will experience. In other words, will the reader be participating as the character or watching as the character or looking down at the tale as God, so to speak?

There are basically three types of POV. They are <u>FIRST</u>, <u>SECOND</u>, and <u>THIRD</u>. But it really gets a little more complicated. All three of them have what I like to call a knowledge factor. This is called *Omniscience* and it comes in varying degrees. There are four layers of omniscience: <u>Omniscient</u>, <u>Objective</u>, <u>Subjective</u>, and <u>Limited</u>.

If you think that last paragraph was a lot of gobbledygook, let me attempt some clarification. For those who are much older, remember back to your elementary school days and those horrible recitations of "I say, you say, he she or it says; we say, you say, they say" as we conjugated our verbs. There was singular and there was plural. Hopefully the following table will help.

	1st PERSON	2nd PERSON	3rd PERSON
SINGULAR	I, me, myself, my	you, your, yourself, yours	he, she, it, his, her(s), its, him, himself, herself, itself
PLURAL	we, us, our, ours, ourselves	you, your, yours, yourselves	they, them, theirs, themselves

Most people will write their story using either 1st person or 3rd person and singular. Very seldom does one use plural and only certain books would consider using 2nd person. What type of book uses 2nd? Basically a which-way book is where you are guided to a point, being told what YOU are doing.

As stated, there are four forms of Omniscience and each of them have their own pros and cons for both the reader and narrator.

<u>Omniscient</u>: The narrator sees and knows everything that is happening with each character and therefore can analyze the thoughts

and emotions of said characters. Many consider this the "God" complex since the narrator has total control over the chronology of the tale by moving forward or backwards as needed to fill in details and reveal to the reader the outcome of such actions.

Objective: The narrator is an observer only; the proverbial 'fly on the wall' reporter. The narrator cannot enter the mind of the character or know what they are thinking.

Subjective: This is a limited narrator who can only reveal what a single character knows and only see what they see.

Limited: Here the narrative story is dualized between Omniscient and Subjective. The narrator can only reveal the story from the one character's viewpoint. The narrator can 'head hop' to different characters but only reveal what that character knows.

So now you realize not only is there 1st, 2nd and 3rd POV but also a plurality AND a knowledge factor. So how does one tie it all together?

	1st PERSON	3rd PERSON
Omniscient	Narration is God-like; all seeing, all knowing, all places. *The Good*: As a writer you can be all characters, revealing all plans. *The Bad*: There are NO secrets; even the bad guy tells all because if s/he doesn't reveal it outright, the mental notes are exposed to the reader.	Even here the narrator floats above, dictating what will be. *The Good*: Complex plots are easier to write by revealing items and viewpoints. *The Bad*: Sometimes there is a lack of focus due to the free-wheeling by the writer.
Objective	In this POV, the writer is more like a reporter who is in the story but not part of the story. The author tells what is happening as if there. *The Good*: The reader is more of a sleuth or detective rather than a	This POV is best suited for a novel and storytelling. The facts are given and revealed but not acted upon by the author. *The Good*: This allows the

		character of the novel. *The Bad*: More telling by the narrator than action by the character.	author to detail items and create intrigue or mystery. *The Bad*: The narrator is stopped from interpreting the facts BUT the reader has the ability to do with the given information.
Subjective		1st person POV is best written in this style as it allows "I" to control the content knowledge. *The Good*: This permits the storyteller to be an active part of the story and also allows the reader to know the character better. *The Bad*: The storyteller is limited to only being able to tell what the current character immediately knows and sees. The character can be literally painted into a corner for lack of knowing what is happening beyond their scope.	This POV is very similar to 1st person with one slight difference; there is a tie between the character and the reader rather than being connected. *The Good*: The writer can manipulate the reader in the POV, for better or worse. *The Bad*: You are bound to one person and must remain true to the events for that period.
Limited		This is used mostly for SF, fantasy and the horror genres; otherwise it is shunned by the others.	This particular POV is custom made for writers as it allows them to jump around from character to character revealing ideas, plots and viewpoints. *The Good*: This allows the writer loopholes of omniscience without truly being omniscient. *The Bad*: The reader can lose focus. If the writer does too much head

		hopping, the reader gets confused about who they are.

As you probably noticed, the above was all done for Singular. Plural POV is awkward and difficult, if not almost impossible to pull off properly.

I hope this has cleared up some aspects of POV.

WEEK 26:

Dumb Writer Edits

I'm not attempting to be snide or in any way rude but let's face it, when we write our first pass, our minds aren't editing or even thinking. Most of us are just trying to get the words on the paper. Therefore we miss some simple edit rules which are going to probably bring down the word count when we go back and start the edits.

How so? Simple.

He stood up. She sat down. They glanced over at the desk. He nodded his head.

In just those four sentences are FIVE useless words which need to be removed -- hence, word count drop!

Let me explain...

When you stand -- normally you stand UP. Only a military command to stand down would make logical sense. So when you state "*He stood.*" your character would stand UP, therefore it isn't necessary to state UP.

The same holds true for sat down. When was the last time you sat up -- again, unless you were in a disciplinary or military type situation where they expect you to sit up with a straight back, and to state it is unnecessary. So, therefore the "*She sat down.*" can be cut to just "she sat" to make it easier for you and the reader.

The next one is a sly one for me. I see action and therefore I would '*glance over at*' whatever but in reality, a person glances at. The "over" is superfluous. Get rid of it. Forget the word "over" is in your dictionary.

And finally the last one. Oooh, and a sneaky one, too. "*He nodded his head.*" If he nodded, it would be his head. You don't nod somebody else's head and just when was the last time you nodded your shoulder or knee? At this moment, let me slip another pet-peeve of mine for editing. *"I like this," she thought to herself.* Really? (Yes, I'm being snide!) How often do you think to somebody else? So it would be "she thought." with the "to herself" as a given. Each of these edits remove an extra TWO words from your word count every time you use them.

I did those edits on a 76k WIP -- and lost almost 3k words. It was a bit unnerving but when I evaluated (I was going to say stood back... but again...) the revised sentences were stronger and the story, as a whole, read much better.

Be sure to read my "That As•Ing•Ly" tip for more great edit tricks.

By Zombies

"That's passive voice!" With that, my editor slashed away at the document using her red pen with wild abandon.

It looked right to me and it sounded okay. My whole body screamed "So who cares?"

I attended a seminar with one of the offered sessions being something like "about Active vs. Passive Voice" so I decided to sit in. The speaker bounced across the front of the classroom in near ecstasy, expounding on the failings of a passive voice story.

I was poised to ask a question when another brave soul interrupted the speaker and asked bluntly, "Who really cares?"

Dust motes froze in time. Those fuzzy balls in the corners snickered. Yes, it was that silent in the room you could actually hear them.

"Why, your reader cares." Her eyes reminded me of those children's paintings from the 1960s, the ones with the large eyes.

I nonchalantly scuffled around in my seat so my poised hand now rested in my lap... nobody the wiser that I considered the identical question. Like the others in the classroom - I stared, shocked, at the hapless victim who asked an innocent question.

With hands flailing in the air, the speaker ranted. *"Your reader wants action! Your reader wants to be included. There is no reason to tell your reader, let them experience the moment."*

Huh?

It's simple! In Active Voice, the subject of the line does the action. In Passive Voice, the sentence is turned around. Simply put:

- Active: Jack hates Jill.
- Passive: Jill is hated by Jack.

It is really easy to tell Passive from Active. Usually (almost always) the sentence is definitely more concise when it is Active Voice.

Now, as I learned just a few short weeks ago. The easiest way to decide if a sentence is active or passive is very simple.

Add "by zombies" after the verb

- Ralph earned an A in school.
- Ralph was given an A in school.
- An A was given to Ralph

Now revisit the sentences, adding "by zombies" as suggested.

- Ralph earned *by zombies* an A in school **OR** Ralph earned an A in school *by zombies*.
- Ralph was given *by zombies* an A in school **OR** Ralph was given an A in school *by zombies*.
- An A was given *by zombies* to Ralph **OR** An A was given to Ralph *by zombies*.

Yes, I know these zombies are very busy creatures but they serve their purpose.

The first sentence is Active Voice and when mutated with "by zombies" it makes no sense or, at least, very little sense.

The next two sentences are both Passive Voice and you can see how well the additive "by zombies" fits into the sentence structure.

So, in the future, when in doubt about whether or not your sentence structure is Active or Passive Voice -- just call on the zombies to help you out. Everyone knows zombies are always looking for live action!

He Said, She Said

Yes, I took the title of a movie from 1991 starring Kevin Bacon and Elizabeth Perkins for my tip this week, but the movie isn't what this article is about.

He said. She said. Ah, yes. SAID. That innocuous word supposedly just disappears when you are reading. It does IF you're not reading it aloud.

I attended a writers' meeting with a guest speaker who wanted to read to us from one of her favorite books and by an author she worshipped. It was lengthy, about 4 pages. I don't remember the book, the author, absolutely nothing except the repetitious "said" being spoken almost every other sentence. Talk about annoying. The speaker apologized, saying she'd never read that segment aloud before... and assured us she probably never would again.

So, yes, the 'said' word will disappear within our mind but it cannot hide from our ears. Therefore, what is a writer to do? Characters have to talk. Learn to write better dialogue. That doesn't mean using another word to replace said. Even using words like replied, quoted, sputtered, snapped, huffed, whispered, etc. will get nauseating, too.

The following are some examples. The original is in regular font, the corrected version is in italics.

"Let me open the door," Janice said and hurried up the steps.
"Let me open the door." Janice hurried ahead and up the steps.

"Do you cook?" Janice asked before sitting in the plush chair.
"Yes, I do," Betty replied, eyeing the diminutive kitchen. "My, everything is right within reach."
"Do you cook?" Janice slumped into the plush chair.
"Yes, I do." Betty eyed the diminutive kitchen. "My, everything is right within reach."

"You have a lovely home," she said while following the older woman to the sun room.
"You have a lovely home." She followed the older woman to the sun room.

"This car is a total piece of junk," John said and threw the wrench to the ground.

71

"This car is a total piece of junk." John threw the wrench to ground in total frustration.

As you can see in each of the examples above, the word "said" was removed and the dialogue tag was changed slightly to accommodate the action. If you were to read the dialogue aloud, the supposedly innocuous word would definitely be missing but yet, the conversation would still sound true.

I'm not recommending the removal of ALL 'said' tags or its relatives — 'replied' and gang, but you definitely can cut several from your dialogue so it doesn't read like he said, she said, he said, she said, ad nausea. As I have stated several times in other tips, when in doubt, read it out loud. You'll be amazed at what you hear—or wished you hadn't heard.

⁂

WEEK 29:

POV Revisited - Part 1

Exactly what is POV? Well, I looked it up and found a whole mess of definitions for the acronym.

- Privately Owned Vehicle
- Power of Veto
- Proof of Value
- Point of Variability
- Peak Operating Voltage
- Port of Vancouver (Vancouver, WA)
- Point of View
- + 86 more...

When I started my research I didn't realize exactly how much information was going to assail me. To make things clearer, I revisited the search engine and looked for "POV writing" and was still amazed at the return but at least this time it was what I wanted.

Writing POV comes in several options. Today's tip will start the discussion of First Person POV. This is represented by the easiest pronoun known to man -- "I" and if not properly executed, can become an ugly mess.

The best way to describe First Person POV is to understand FOV (Field of View) and AOE (Area of Expertise) of your character. Using FOV -- imagine yourself sitting at a window looking at the front yard, the street and a couple of neighbor's homes. That is your field of view. You can only see a small segment of the world. Unless you lean out the window, only with some stretching and bending will you be able to see a very large area. You can only see and relate to what you see in your small FOV. If your window looks out on the back yard, you have no knowledge of what is happening in the front or side yards.

There is a loophole. You can't see what is happening but you can hear. There are people in a pool in the side yard and the sound of the mower running in the front yard. BUT, you have no idea if the young lady is wearing a skimpy black bikini or if the lawn mower is 0-turn radius type.

Now add Area of Expertise. Remember that pool? Of course you do, you blew the stupid thing up by yourself. It was a yellow and purple plastic thing. And that mower? Hearing the engine backfire assures you it is the neighbor's very old Cub Cadet rider and the mower blades whine when going up and down inclines.

BUT! You need to let your reader know this information before you reveal it. See example...

Example 1: *I sat at the open window looking out on the garden. In the distance I could hear kids splashing about in the new yellow and purple plastic pool. My neighbor mowed his front yard with the old Cub Cadet.*

Example 2: *I sat at the open window looking out on the garden. In the distance I could hear my kids playing in their new pool. I just hoped they didn't break the inflated tubes since it took me almost 3 hours to blow it up. The yellow tube was small and filled quickly but the purple tube was much bigger and took a long time. I also could hear my neighbor labor up and down the hilly front yard with the old Cub Cadet. No matter how much we worked on it, the mower continued to backfire and the blades always whined on the inclines.*

The first example is a poor demonstration of First Person POV. The character is giving us information that s/he can only guess about. S/he can't see the pool and therefore can't really know it is yellow and purple. Hearing the mower could be the neighbor's but it could also be the spouse or a child using the mower. S/he can't see the action and, therefore, can't describe it.

In First Person POV -- if the character can't touch, taste or see the item, the character can't describe it. Yes, First Person POV is extremely restrictive, yet, at the same time, it allows the reader to become very personal with the character. They meld as one.

Remember that pronoun I mentioned? I? Okay, by using "me, myself, and I" as the character, you are no longer leading the reader, you ARE the reader. So I am seeing this, I am doing that, things are happening to me! In First Person POV, you can't get any more personal and intimate with your reader.

There is no "Goose bumps rippled his arms, sending chills down his back." Now it is "Goose bumps rippled my arms, sending chills down my back." Suddenly the reader realizes, yes, indeed, there are goose bumps and feels those chills. He shudders. By using First Person POV you can really scare the be-Jesus out of your readers and make them squirm.

They are no longer standing outside the action, watching. They are in the action and it is happening to them.

If properly written and executed, using First Person POV can leave your reader breathless, heart-pumping excited and turning pages very quickly.

Next time we will continue with First Person POV.

POV Revisited - Part 2

Welcome back. Now let's delve a little more into 1st person POV. I would like to explain AOE (Area of Expertise) a little more in detail. It is the knowledge factor and I like to think there are four categories within it.

They are: *Omniscient, Objective, Subjective, Limited*. A more detailed explanation follows:

Omniscient: The narrator sees and knows everything that is happening with each character and therefore can analyze the thoughts and emotions of said characters. Many consider this the "God" complex since the narrator has total control over the chronology of the tale by moving forward or backwards as needed to fill in details and reveal to the reader the outcome of such actions.

Objective: The narrator is an observer only—the proverbial 'fly on the wall' reporter. The narrator cannot enter the mind of the character or know what they are thinking.

Subjective: This is a limited narrator who can only reveal what a single character knows and only see what they see.

Limited: Here the narrative story is dualized between Omniscient and Subjective. The narrator can only reveal the story from the one character's viewpoint. The narrator can 'head hop' to different characters but only reveal what that character knows.

So how does this apply to 1st Person POV?

Omniscient: Narration is God-like; all seeing, all knowing, all places.
The Good: As a writer you can be all characters, revealing all plans.
The Bad: There are NO secrets; even the bad guy tells all because if s/he doesn't reveal it outright, the mental notes are exposed to the reader.

Objective: In this POV, the writer is more like a reporter who is in the story but not part of the story. The author tells what is happening as if there.
The Good: The reader is more of a sleuth or detective rather than a character of the novel.

The Bad: More telling by the narrator than action by the character.

Subjective: 1st person POV is best written in this style as it allows "I" to control the content knowledge.
The Good: This permits the storyteller to be an active part of the story and also allows the reader to know the character better.
The Bad: The storyteller is limited to only being able to tell what the current character immediately knows and sees. The character can be literally painted into a corner for lack of knowing what is happening beyond their scope.

Limited: This is used mostly for SF, fantasy and the horror genres; otherwise it is shunned by the others.
The Good: Very tight POV where the reader is the character.
The Bad: All information must be fed to the character/reader and too often it becomes an "info dump" and bores the reader.

Each writer must decide what POV s/he will use when creating the next masterpiece. The hard part is making sure to stay in that POV for the entire book. Good luck.

A Good Writer

What makes a good writer? A good story? A good plot? Great dialogue? Timing? Exactly what is it?

All of the above are possibilities. Strangely, good spelling should be on that list. Why? Simple.

The pale sit in the middle of the for foot bye ate foot area. Open two the knight, the do glistened like to ore moor diamonds as they fell their two the flower-coated floor.

Yes, a terrible story and even worse spelling. You should be able to find at least THIRTEEN errors above.

The [pale] pail sit in the middle of the [for] four foot [bye] by [ate] eight foot area. Open [two] to the [knight,] night, the [do] dew glistened like [to] two [ore] or [moor] more diamonds as they fell [their] there [two] to the [flower] flour-coated floor.

I enjoy reading but I hate finding incorrect spellings for words. We all know those words, the homophones. They sound alike but are spelled differently.

Everyone is familiar with homonyms - those words that are spelled the same but have different meanings like:

- bear: (1) tolerate, (2) an animal

- fair: (1) carnival, (2) free from bias

- dock: (1) a pier, (2) deduct wages; (3) shorten a tail

The dictionary is full of them, as is our language. Then there are the homophones. Those are what I used above and they are the most notorious beasts of the spelling dilemma.

- to: a direction; two: a number; too: also

- for: a purpose; four: a number; fore: a yell

- their: owned by a group; there: a place; they're: a conjunction of they and are

- pale: to lack color; pail: a bucket

- or: otherwise; ore: raw metal; oar: a paddle

• knight: a mounted warrior; night: dark segment of a day

You, as a writer, must use the correctly spelled word or your tale of wonder may become just that -- a tale of wonder.

The pail of the night.

If you meant "pale" which signifies colorless, then yes, it can add a depth of darkness or fear. But, you used "pail" which indicates something totally different such as a "relief" station for the bladder or...

There is a difference between "rein," "rain," and "reign." To write "His rain of terror..." really makes the reader question exactly what image you are attempting to project. Making sure you use the correct spelling will increase the chances your reader will enjoy the story even more rather than questioning the meaning or laughing at the image the incorrect spelling brought to mind.

A good writer knows how to spell. If in doubt, look it up.

It's your tern, do with it as you see fit.

Actually, I meant, it is your TURN, do with it as you fit. Although, if you truly do own a tern, it is yours and you may do with it as you wish.

What's In A Job Title?

Yes, it is a strange title for a writing tip but a very important one. Yes, you are an author, a writer, etc. but this article is about, not necessarily you, but your character. Did that catch you off-guard?

Jane ambled through the house, dusting this and that as she went. House work!

Is Jane a house wife? You've heard the phrase "I'm just a house wife." Actually, in today's society, Jane is a Domestic Engineer.

Take this example as a better one...

Stuart opened the frosted glass door to the office and noticed the young lady behind the desk. He ambled up to her. "I'm here to see, Mr. Smith."

She glanced up from her nails. "I'm Mr. Smith's administrative assistant. May I inquire as to your business with Mr. Smith?"

Hmm? Somehow that detective story took a turn you didn't expect.

So, what am I talking about? I'm talking about title-fluffing. It has become more prevalent in the last two decades than ever before. In 1950 it was common for a man to say he worked in an office. Then, for some reason, it became popular for a man to drop a 'title' to designate his work environment. Well, part of the reason for title fluffing was to make the employee feel better about himself, especially when he wasn't getting a raise. Still, going from office worker to Time Keeper didn't put more meat and potatoes on the table.

Using the bank as an example...

There was the President, Vice-President, Secretary, and bank tellers. Now there is the Chief Executive Officer, President of Finances, President of Loans, President of Accounts and of course, each of them have Vice-Presidents. They no longer have secretaries but Administrative Assistants and Receptionists. Even bank tellers have fancier titles -- Finance Officers, Financial Advisors.

As I grew up, I was a paperboy. Today that is known as a Media Distribution and Account Collections Agent. Really? When I was a janitor for a company (a short-term job) they actually told me I would be a

Sanitation Consultant. Somehow, while I was scrubbing the porcelain throne, I didn't feel like a consultant. Never once in the three weeks I performed as a Sanitation Consultant, did I consult with patrons of the restroom nor did I suggest stall 2 over stall 5. By the way, I moved from that position to one titled "Financial Inventory Distributor." Yeah, I was a clerk at the cash register for the grocery store. I won't go into the other positions available such as General Manager who oversaw the following people—Manager: Produce, Manager: Meats, Manager: Domestics, Manager: Pharmacy, etc. I believe there was probably about ten or twelve different managers. Stock boys were Inventory Specialists.

So exactly what does all this title fluffing have to do with writing? You may want to make sure that you don't degrade or berate your character by saying s/he was 'just a teller' or 'housewife' or 'paperboy.' You may want to colorize your writing with the new titles.

Just think how much better Jane will appear to your reader as a Domestic Engineer than a regular housewife. Brandy, the greeter at a fine restaurant is now a Reservation Specialist. And Jackie in the cloakroom is no longer a hat/coat check girl but a Garment Technician.

Maybe I'm getting old but, for me, the idea of writing "harried housewife" vs. "harried domestic engineer" gives me two different images. Housewife I see in dress, maybe a bandana wrapped around her curler-infused hair, a small child in one arm and the vacuum cleaner in the other. A domestic engineer just seems too stiff, like a woman wearing a suit and somehow the vacuum cleaner doesn't seem to be part of the uniform. Fine, call me politically incorrect but some of these new titles just don't cut it in the writing world.

So, you're the writer - what is your job title? That's simple: Title Procurement Officer. Your job is to decide what occupation each character in your story will have and how they will exist handling their title. Have fun.

The Editing Process

You have finished your masterpiece and it is now ready to be sent out to publishers... NOT!

It is amazing how many new writers think that once they have placed the words to paper that the process is done and now is the time to send it off the publisher. They are so wrong. There are several steps to the writing of a novel: Creation, Continuity, Creativity, Reality, Finality.

You wrote the novel. That was the creative process. You created a manuscript. It is now a tangible item but it is in its purest, raw form. That manuscript is in no way ready for publication. In fact, it really isn't even ready to be presented to anyone!

Your document - within the realms of your own mind - is the most fantastic, well-written, next best-seller... or at least you think it is. Unfortunately, trust me, it isn't.

Now is the time to go back through the story and look at your plots and sub-plots. Did you satisfactorily tie-up the loose ends on each of them? Or are there dangling issues that need to be addressed? Having Jack find that 800 caret diamond in the cave is a stroke of pure luck. So what purpose did it serve? Why an 800 caret diamond? Other than Jack sticking it in his pocket, what happened? Or how about Julie who thinks Stanley, the president of the chess club, is a cute boy. Did Stanley die? Did they date?

There has to be a reason for everything (so I've been told) and if you mentioned something, you should resolve it.

Jack used the diamond to cut through a giant 3 inch glass wall. When it shattered after being scratched by the diamond, a shard hit his hand and he dropped the diamond and it was lost. As for Stanley, our heroine thinks he is dreamy but discovers Stanley is gay.

So once you're done writing, you go back through the work to make sure all the loose ends are finalized. But, you're not done. As you go through the work you realize that for Jack, the shattering glass crumbled the thin cave floor and he fell into a larger cavern below.

Ah-ha! You've hit upon Creativity. As you go through fixing things you discover new opportunities, twists and turns for the story to make it even more robust and thrilling.

Finally you come to realize that at some point you need to face facts. Reality. It has three faces.

<u>Face 1</u>: The sheer size of Jack's diamond would make it difficult to carry in a pocket. Or Julie's infatuation with Stanley could actually be better for the story, so Stanley is no longer gay. That is part of the reality.

<u>Face 2</u>: You now know that somebody else needs to read this work. In other words, you are looking for edits. So you have your mom, your friends, you neighbors and maybe even your local writing group buddies take a crack at making sure the story is good, the spelling is correct and everything is falling into place properly.

<u>Face 3</u>: You need a real editor, somebody who knows what they are doing to address the writing itself.

Now you are approaching Finality. The last stage of editing. This is where you receive back a heavily marked and scribbled upon document, totally destroying your psyche. Are you truly a writer?

Editing is a process that can take several weeks to several months. Editing isn't just making sure that the words are spelled correctly or that the punctuation has been properly assigned. Editing is looking at the document and evaluating the contents, validating the POV, verifying plots, subplots and storyline for continuity. Editing is a process that you can do up to a point.

At some point, whether you want to believe it or not, you will need to have another person edit your work. This should be somebody who is not familiar with your current work so any surprises, plots, etc are properly addressed.

As the author, you are too close to the work. In your head you know all the details and if one is missing in the text, it is in your mind's eye and therefore, must also be in the tale. Or you may have deleted a scene that revealed the size of the diamond and to say it was too large later seems to come in from nowhere, the blind side, per se.

Bottom line: Never ever submit a raw work.

The Writer's Stream

Each day a writer will wake up and like any other work person, go to work which means sitting at the desk, or where ever it is they wish to work that day, before the computer, laptop or maybe even a real typewriter, and start typing.

Exactly how does a writer put the text to the proverbial paper?

Simple.

Word thought stream.

In the back of the writer's mind is a small projector that flashes either images or full-blown scenes which are then put down for all prosperity. Well, that is, after a major amount of editing later.

Sometimes a writer will only see a small segment of the whole plan and need to slowly explore the possibilities. Think of it as a maze. You see the entrance. From that point on, it is trial and error to get to the finish line.

Oh, wouldn't that be nice? Start at the beginning and work toward the end? It doesn't normally happen that way. Usually a writer is dropped off in the maze somewhere -- just a couple of corners from the entrance or end or sometimes in the middle or anywhere else within the maze. The only problem is - the writer doesn't know where, in the maze, s/he is. What fun exploring.

OR, the writer is given a log where, hidden within the bark encrusted fifty foot tall redwood tree trunk, the writer must whittle it down to discover that small trophy about the size of an Oscar Award.

This is what word thought stream is all about. A writer working his or her way through a giant sea of words, finding in this morass just the perfect word for the reader to grasp onto and enjoy.

What does this mean? Simple. A writer can type "Andrea opened the car door. She slid across the back seat to the middle." Or the writer can type "Andrea opened the car's back door then scooted across to the middle."

Both are correct but one is more succinct. The stream could or would be the first example while in the final version, the last sentence more than likely would make the cut.

The stream is to get the words written, not necessarily in their final version, but in a rough, image-driven, rush to the end.

NaNoWriMo (National Novel Writing Month) is about such a method. It is about getting 50,000 words written in 30 days. It is about letting your mind go free and allowing it to get the words, the concepts and ideas, down and then going back over all of it at a later date.

DID YOU CATCH THE CAVEAT?

...going back over all of it at a later date.

A writing stream is all about getting the text out of your mind and either on paper or cyber-storage of a disk. It is not about making sure you have exact, right word. You want the instant image recorded. This is the writing process. The editing process is going back checking for the correct word choice. It is much easier to go back and add "Hell's inferno of mesmerizing flames licking the building's walls." On the fly, in the heat of the writing moment, "licking flames of Hell" will suffice.

Also, since NaNoWriMo only requires 50k and most novels should be in the 65-95k size, taking those 4 words and expanding to 9 words helps to extend the word count.

Again, word thought stream is about getting the words down. It is about getting the idea from the brain to paper. A writer who creates a work with 45-60k words in 30 days can use the next 6-9 months getting those words to be more engaging.

Yes, a good writer can easily produce a novel each year. Some can even write two novels a year.

Learn to use word thought stream.

⁇

WEEK 35:

August! The Christmas Rush Is Over

So hard to believe, isn't it? Already in August and the Christmas rush is over. How? If you haven't sent your holiday-themed story to a magazine by the end of June, mid-July at latest, then you've missed the opportunity to get it published in the December issue.

Well, not totally, but perhaps.

Several electronic magazines can usually hold off until November, at the extreme latest, for a holiday-themed story. Surprisingly, many of them are now opting for a longer lead-in time period and you may find yourself out-in-the-cold when trying to hustle that last minute Christmas holiday story on December 3rd.

Yes, it is August and you might be surprised to discover that any Valentine-themed story might be pushing the deadlines of the paper industry magazines.

A writer doesn't want to rely strictly on the electronic world to save him or her. Remember, many of the paper magazines now do electronic publishing and therefore need to match their paper counterparts. Any large magazine that has an electronic version, must deal with the paper version and have the electronic edition match as closely as possible. Hence, it must also deal with deadlines and due dates.

This is why some of the magazines offer the electronic version with 'specials' for their customers. These 'specials' are those last minute items the editor feels needed to be in but can no longer put it into the print edition. Hence, if you're lucky enough to gain access to such a coveted spot, more power to you.

So exactly how does a paper magazine establish due dates? Look at it this way:

Due Date | Magazine Issue

June 30 | December (Christmas/Chanukah/Kwanzaa)

July 31 | January (New Years/Martin Luther King Day)

August 31 | February (Valentines/Presidents' Day)

September 30 | March (St. Patrick's Day)

October 31 | April (Tax Day/April Fools Day)

November 30 | May (Memorial Day)

December 31 | June (Summer/Vacation)

January 31 | July (4th of July/Vacation)

February 28/29 | August (End of Summer/School Return)

March 31 | September (Labor Day/School)

April 30 | October (Halloween/Fall)

May 31 | November (Thanksgiving/pre-Holiday)

The above is only a suggestion. To verify actual due dates, as always, the writer must seek out the guidelines of the magazine. Some magazines will desire only a 30-90 day lead while others may want a 9 month lead. Always, ALWAYS check guidelines.

Another aspect to consider is if the magazine (both online and/or paper) has a theme for the issue. A definite No-No is submitting a story about the basics of Kwanzaa when the issue will be themed about "Tieing Up Chanukah" and deciding which is the proper tie to give.

So, do you remember that cute little story you wrote right after the holidays? Now is the time to get it cleaned up and maybe, just maybe, a little holiday magic will allow you to find a place to submit and get accepted. Time is running out, but you can still try.

How To Write Better and Faster

Everyone wants to write a complete novel in the least amount of time. Some say a weekend (not enough coffee in the world for me to do that!) while others say 30 days (National Novel Writing Month – www.nanowrimo.org) and even more claim it takes three to six months or longer.

I have done the 30 day challenge several times, failing only the first time. In my defense, I attempted to do a cookbook and it was the year my dad passed away less than 30 days prior to the event. Just not a good combination, but the learning experience was great.

There are some simple rules to make writing better and faster. They are:

- Outline
- Research
- Write simple
- Audience
- Know English
- Read Aloud

Let's examine each aspect -- just a little.

Outline: I have found outlining to be a way to keep me on target but I also know that if a certain story line strays on a tangent, sometimes it is worth the visit to see where it will go. I was able to add almost five chapters to a novel just by letting the story tell itself rather than forcing it into the square I'd designed. So, outlines are a guide but they aren't carved in stone. If a story changes, if following an outline, remember, there are sub-categories with outlining. Use them. I like to claim I use clay and don't let it dry out, but in reality, I use a word processor and table layout, adding rows and columns as necessary to accommodate the alterations. By the way, that stray of five chapters allowed me a twist I'd missed and a very powerful ending - much better than the one I'd originally planned.

Research: Know what you write. Research will help you gain that edge. I like to call it "instant Einstein" because I will study my subject matter and get quite knowledgeable while I am writing. Of course, three to four months later, I have some facts locked into my brain tissue, but the rest has dribbled out through the sieve I call my cranial matter. For my novel *Three Steps: The Journeys of Ayrold* I found myself off on so many different research areas. I filled two binders with information. Some of the potions and chants are based on actual concoctions. I just tweaked them for my usage.

Write Simple: One word can replace a thousand if it is the right word. An example: *John joined Jim, Pete, Paul and Tom at the table. He took the seat in the middle with Jim and Paul to his left and Pete and Tom to his right.*

The rewrite: *John joined the others at the table. He took the middle seat between the four men.*

Yes, word count definitely got clobbered but better to have tight writing than superfluous fluff words. The rewrite was tighter and gave the exact same impression as the original, the only difference was the names. Who cares about who sat on the left and right? Publishers want to pay for solid writing, not extra words. So when you write, use the KISS method - Keep It Seriously Simple or Keep It Simple Stupid, your call.

Audience: So, you are writing a book about zombies who attack the aliens who are invading the planet only to be eluded by the humans who used star travel to escape. So who is your audience? Zombie lovers? Science fiction? Space fiction? Is it horror? The list can continue on and on but the bottom line is easy. Who is your audience? What target audience are you hoping to have read this masterpiece? Knowing who you want to read the story will help you to write the story and keep it on track. Deciding it will be a zombie story and about half way through realizing you might want it to be more science fiction can muddle your tale. And whatever you do, don't decide to throw in a romance between a zombie and alien at the very last minute.

Know English: This will definitely help you to write better and faster, especially if you are hoping to publish in the English language. BUT, if you are a German, writing a German story, well, then, know German or whatever language you are planning to get your story published. If you know the words beyond the basics of "Yo!" and "How'ya doing" as a greeting, dialogue will glow and write itself. Also, by knowing English, you must also know how to spell. I mean, *like a rider really kneads two spell awl the words correckly.* Trust me, it helps. By the way, my built-in spell checker only found ONE word as spelled incorrectly. There were definitely more.

<u>Read Aloud</u>: This is one of the best rule of thumb for any writer. Always take the time to read your piece aloud. I know it sounds stupid and like a waste of time but if you read each word aloud, you will hear exactly how it sounds. Believe me, in our mind, the text flows beautifully and is very eloquent. When spoken aloud, certain words will come to surface repeatedly and any awkwardness of the sentence's structure will come to light. The best editor, before paying the "big bucks" for a professional editor, is sitting alone and reading aloud. Do have a red pen handy to correct the errors. You will discover "he said" and "she said" are not the innocuous and invisible words everyone claims them to be. Variations in sentence structure, or lack of variations, will also become obvious.

I didn't list this one since it is an acquired item. Skill. As you write, and continue to write, you will hone your talent and in turn, gain skill. I have had the horrible pain of going back to read something I wrote several decades earlier. Cringe is an understatement. For the works not published, there is hope to improve them. For those that were published, I question how the submission made it beyond the trash pile, let alone the slush pile. Never, ever go back and read your work from the past. Move forward.

For me, writing is fun. I don't figure it will be a living salary but, as my wife likes to call it, a tidy sum of luxuries. Maybe I will get lucky and have a big seller. I dream of such and any writer who claims otherwise is living in denial. I want to see writers move forward and applaud any who make the success route. I will continue to write, striving for excellence.

How Much To Pay For Edits

I was asked "How much should a new writer pay for edits and how many edits should be done?" My flip answer is simple - How deep are your pockets?

Let me first say this: I hate to pay for edits, BUT, I realize my work is not perfect and needs edits.

So, with that in mind, let me explain how I get edits done.

First, I write the novel or story. Then I (that is ME, myself and I - the three of us) go back over and edit as much as feasibly possible. I correct words, punctuation, spelling, line structure, repetitious words, weak verbs and whatever else I see.

Now I send it out to my select group of reader/editors. Each person in this collective serves a different purpose.

Person #1 really tears into my work and edits with a strong arm: going over my spelling, punctuation, word choices. She leaves a trail of red you won't believe.

Person #2 doesn't like to offend so he really reads it more for content, context, and continuity. If something doesn't make sense to him or he doesn't follow the flow, he lets me know.

Person #3 is one who is outside the genre of the story. I know that doesn't make sense but he reads the story and lets me know what works and doesn't work. It is a strange idea but I figure if somebody who normally doesn't read, let's say, science fiction, and is given a SF novel. There will be valid feedback.

Person #4 is one who I use from the start as I bounce ideas and plots off her and give her small vignettes to read as I write. She is very busy but can read a page or two without too much difficulty and give me feedback.

As you can see, each person actually does edits but the one really gets into the nitty-gritty while the others notate those glaring errors. Surprisingly, not everyone catches the same errors.

These are friends. They do this for free. Okay, in return, I do edits for them and read for plot, continuity, etc.

Anyway, once I get back their edits, I go into my WIP and see what I can fix. Remember, this is YOUR story and therefore, any suggested fixes are your decision to make. So, I do adjustments then I take one last pass at the story. I read it aloud! Slowly. Enunciating each word. This has to be done so your ears can hear. I realize this sounds silly to new writers, but trust me, your mind reads more than it sees. I read a sentence four times and it wasn't until I read it aloud that I could hear just how trite and awkward it truly sounded. If it sounds good spoken aloud, it will read even better in the mind.

NOW I pay the big bucks to a professional editor. Yes, I do professional editing but I'm not an idiot. As they say, any man who attempts to defend himself, has a fool for a lawyer. The same holds true for editing. Therefore, I put my final work into the hands of another professional who will be seeing it for the first time with an unprejudiced mind.

I jokingly claim my editor buys her ink in 55 gallon barrels and uses it freely. The first time I used her, I swear that some of the returned pages had more red ink than black ink. Not so today, almost fifteen years later. Nonetheless, she does use a lot of red ink.

Now for the important, million dollar question. How much? This is something that you, as an author, must decide since only you know your financial situation. There are editors who charge by the hour, by the word, by the page, and several other methods. Evaluate each method against your particular piece. Dependent upon the method, the cost could work out to be anywhere from $.50 a page to $15.00 a page or $40.00 for a manuscript to $4000.00.

Be sure to check out the editor, read the reviews, ask for references, etc. etc. Remember, this is YOUR money. I had a friend pay over $1,000 for edits. When she got the manuscript back, there were a total of approximately 300 corrections over the 500 pages -- mostly spelling and punctuation fixes. The editor's comment: good story, nice plot - ready to go. She sent it out and the first publisher was nice enough to respond back with: Good story. Too many characters and locales. Seek professional editing service.

She joined a writing group where I was a member and I saw the manuscript for the first time after it had come back from the publisher. She had over 100 characters and 22 locales, names that rhymed or were spelled almost alike. When I read the story, I was totally lost and confused, unable to keep characters at bay or remember which location they were at as she bounced between the 20+ places.

My editor offers a dual editing special. A person can be edited once through for $X OR that person can choose what she likes to call "double" edit. She edits, returns, you fix, send back to her for 2nd edit which she does and returns to you. The best way to describe this method would be something like -- $2/page for once through edits or $3/page for double edit. You pay for the double edit up front at the start.

So, how much or how many edits does an author want? As many as feasibly possible is the obvious answer. How many do they want to pay for? Zero, but reality is -- as many as necessary to get the manuscript to be a publishable product.

Your readers deserve a solid, final product.

[?]

Mr. Thesaurus, If You Please...

What's another word for "raced" in a sentence like — He raced to the house?

During the first pass of writing your story, you slap whatever word immediately comes to mind to describe the action. Okay, that's what I do, since much of my writing is done as scenes within my mind. I love watching movies, even those I am making up as I write.

So, calling on Mr. Thesaurus at www.thesaurus.com, we can easily discover several words to replace "race" such as: chase, run, sprint, dash, go, rush, scurry. But there is also scramble, surge, charge, hasten, hurried plus many more — if you take the time to search a little further into possibilities for words like 'rush,' or 'dash.'

I just finished going over the "professional edits" on my latest work. The editor took exception to everyone "racing" here and there. I believe she nailed me for about 70 "raced" entries.

I read a book a couple of months ago where everyone smiled and nodded their heads. My characters do a lot of that, too. I found other actions for my characters. Plus, in addition to smiling, my characters can also smirk, beam, grin, laugh, snicker or they can scowl, frown, and grimace. The options are numerous.

Sometimes, if you look carefully, a properly chosen word can make the scene come alive.

> OK: *He got into the car.* Better: *He slid into the front seat.*
> OK: *She walked into the room.* Better: *She strutted into the assembly.*
> OK: *The small boy ran to first base.* Better: *The lad scampered to first base.*
> OK: *The necklace was shiny and new.* Better: *The necklace glittered in its newness.*

For some writers, going back over their work to clean it up is all about making sure the words are spelled correctly, and that the punctuation is in place. It really should be the writer's chance to punch up the story, change the boring, ho-hum words to a better selection. Don't get me wrong — I'm not telling you to over-glorify the text. There is no reason for flowery prose unless it is appropriate.

Read the following:

The white walls of the cliffs were practically unscalable. The pirates hunted for possible footholds.

The alabaster chalk walls of the sheer cliffs were treacherous. The pirates scoured the base for potential footholds.

Both scenes depict the same, basic image but the 2nd one has more life and vitality. First pass should be the first example. The second and following passes should give your work the polish of example two.

There is no reason to write "The silvery dewdrops glistened like diamond chips as they slid on the emerald path of the blade of grass." Yes, it is descriptive, but exactly where do you feel it would be appropriate? My recommendation? Save all that flowery prose for poetry — where it counts.

So the bottom line is simple: Write tight prose with vivid images. "He rushed to the car." conveys your idea but "He speedily slid into the front seat." swells with images. Don't cheat yourself or your reader.

WEEK 39:

Where's The Caboose?

Remember back ... by the way, I am talking to those over 40 years of age ... when, as a child, you'd sit in the car and watch the train pass in front of you? The crossing lights would flash and soon you'd hear the distant whistle. If you were really lucky - you'd get to hear the Doppler Effect as suddenly, the big locomotive with its horn blaring, charged across your field of vision. You'd start the count as the engine was followed by freight cars, oil tankers, flat bed cars and then the final car. Like a cherry on top of a soda - the caboose whisked away as the train sped down the tracks.

Sometimes, to my delight, a trainman might be riding that car and be standing on the back deck, hanging onto the black railing. I'd wave and if he saw me, he'd wave back.

Today the trains pass in front of my vehicle as I impatiently wait, fingers tapping away on the steering wheel. Suddenly, the last car flicks by and I see a little flashing red light. There is no caboose. No trainman. The train has lost its magic.

Sometimes, our writing is exactly like those trains.

No magic. No caboose.

You've heard the adage: Putting the cart before the horse.

Some do that in their writing.

He closed the front door and waved good bye.

He what? The caboose got moved to the front of the sentence. Yes, the cart is not following the horse, but instead is now pushing the cart. The sentence should read:

He waved good bye and shut the front door.

This is an obvious and glaring example. Others are much more subtle.

Matt's hip burned after he slid down the ravine.

The sentence 'seems' perfectly okay but if you read it closely, the horse (sliding down the ravine) is after the cart (a burning hip) which is awkward. A better construct would be:

96

Matt slid down the ravine's rough wall. His hip burned from the abrasive action.

Splitting the sentence into two segments and getting the proper timeline aligned, you've actually added more description and depth.

Another way to look at this would be -- Action / Result, Response or Reaction.

He yelled bloody murder and grabbed his hand as the car door shut on it.

A better way to write that and put the action first, reaction following it, rather than at the start of the sentence would be:

The car door slammed on his fingers. Aaron screamed bloody murder, yanking his hand away and gingerly attempting to bend them.

Again, by fixing the sentence timeline or putting the horse first, the cart next, you've added more detail and description thereby making a stronger story for the reader.

Of course, if you want to remove the caboose from the train and just have that red flashing light at the end, you can simply write the sentence as:

He slammed his hand in the car door.

You have the action. You don't have the reaction - the caboose - and therefore, are missing a little of the magic. By removing the magic, your reader is cheated.

A train is only as good as the cars that compose it. We love to see the snappy locomotive, the nifty coal car, followed by a mixture of box cars, flat cars, tankers and, finally, at the very end, the car we all love - the caboose with the trainman who waves at us.

Story Continuity

One of the worst sins a writer can commit is to confuse the reader. The easiest way to do this is to have the story's continuity broken.

What exactly is story continuity?

For many, it is just a simple route from point A to point B and everything occurs as a smooth road.

But, in reality, there is more to that than meets the eye and sometimes it is very subtle. For instance, the following scene from a book which takes place at the beginning of 1950:

Billy sat on the floor, watching the Roy Rogers Show on the huge screen. Nellybelle, the Army-green jeep, was, once again, driving away without Pat.

There are three inconsistencies in the above two sentences...

1) maybe some people would consider a 10" screen huge and in 1950 maybe it was, but...
2) color on TV didn't happen until late 50s and then, only the rich had it. Most Americans didn't have color TV until the 60s.
3) this is the most subtle, The Roy Rogers Show didn't air until 1951.

Other inconsistencies which can harm continuity are simple actions. I wrote a tale where two riders were preparing to break camp and get on their horses. I had the one getting on, off, on, off, on, off. As my alpha-reader stated: I'm getting light-headed. Just let him wait until everything is done THEN let him get on his horse.

In a current work, I have an accident happen and the father says: "Daniel, you go to work. Rachel, you help get the kids around and ready for school."

Off-hand it seems okay but there is an issue. Daniel is a student also. School is out and it is Daniel's first day at work. Needless to say, there was a little scurry to straighten out the scene. FYI: Daniel went to work. Rachel got the kids around and they worked in the garden. Whew!

Writing period pieces, whether historical or not, get tricky. With time, things change. So do holidays!

Presidents' Day, Memorial Day, and Columbus Day weren't always on a Monday. In fact, Veterans' Day, observed November 11th was temporarily changed to a Monday and then returned to its proper place where it is now. Still, if you are writing a period piece, the writer must make an effort to be true to the era. Three-day weekends were a rarity in the 50s and 60s unless the specified date fell on a Friday or Monday. There was no Presidents' Day - George Wasington and Abraham Lincoln both had their own day of honor.

Also, some holidays have been added to the calendar. Martin Luther King Day was not observed until 1986. To close a school or business on a Monday in 1973 would be breaking your reader's continuum.

Susie sweeps and cleans the floor. She doesn't clean and sweep the floor. If your character slips to the floor and somebody helps her to a chair. Obviously she can't lean over and rest her hand out on the floor to prop her up.

Continuity is more than getting a person from point A to point B. It is about making sure everything in between is in correct order also.

WEEK 41:

What To Write

Writer's Block!!

Those two words rip into a writer's soul like a fire-edged sword. If you're the writer of horror - it is the moment when the creature suddenly turns to run away. If you're a writer of romance - it is the moment when the hero turns to the love interest and stares blankly.

Each genre has that moment when the writer draws a blank.

I have faced the beast this week in many aspects. The worst, with a looming deadline, was this writing tip. I had no idea of what to write.

So how does one approach this beast and win the battle?

Strangely, the answer is WRITE!

Over the years I discovered the truth of writer's block. It is no more than your tale, article, poem, whatever you're writing, suddenly not going in the direction it should. Your mind is now telling you to step back, analyze then gird yourself for a new attack. You will be richly rewarded in doing this. Sometimes the time necessary to step back can be 5 minutes or it can be 5 hours. It might even be 5 days or 5 weeks. I know one novel I was struggling with took almost 5 years to find the correct path so the story could be told. Talk about writer's block!

Earlier I mentioned the word 'poem' - you probably frowned and let it pass. But, truth be told, even poets get stumped. It may be a phrasing of the words to convey the thought. It could be just finding the right word. In poetry, as in prose, there is a difference between "a tree" and "the tree." Stop and think that one over.

Imagine the chagrin of a poet when he writes "skies of red and orange" and now has to find a rhyming word for orange. To my knowledge, there isn't a match, although there are some words that might be considered--but that's another article.

Writer's block can hit at any moment and usually when you really don't have the time to address it. Hmm? Is there ever a good time for a bad situation? Again, another article.

So, for me, to find a writing tip of use became tantamount. Finally in desperation I asked my wife. I explained I had writer's block and had no idea of what to write. For some reason, my rule didn't fly with the situation this time - I hadn't even started an article, so I knew I couldn't be barking up the wrong tree. She suggested I write about writer's block.

So, the final explanation of how to win the battle with writer's block is answered: Ask your spouse, a friend, your significant other, partner... even a total stranger, if you're brave enough.

I realize this tip seems rather tongue-in-cheek, but if you read it carefully, you'll see there is a mote of knowledge hidden within. If you missed it -- WRITE.

I sat before my computer and began to write. In less than 20 minutes this tip came into existence. Again, the answer was there all the time -- WRITE!

So when you, the writer, are faced with the ugly beast known as Writer's Block, step back, analyze, ask another person, and then attack.

WEEK 42:

What's In A Name?

Naming your characters should be as involved as naming your newborn child - after all, this character just came into existence. So what steps are taken to create this new entity?

First step. How strong is this character in the story? Is s/he a lead, minor (supporting) or incidental (casual walk-on type) individual?

Lead characters should have names that are easy to remember, be strong and fit the personality. Exactly what does that mean? Think of it as Mary Smith. Now exactly how exciting is that name? Does it bring images of adventure? Do you see her as a group leader? Is she the champion you want? Now think about the name Veronica McTaggarty. This name invokes a sense of strength, a leader, a woman who you probably don't want to mess with.

If you're writing a romance novel, your heart-throb lead could be George, Tom or Bob but Angus, Brock, and Caleb once more infuses your mind with a lead man with chiseled features and just the perfect amount of brawn to match the brain.

When you name your child, you agonize over making sure it is the perfect name for your child. So it should be for your story characters.

I wrote some detective mystery stories back when I first became serious about writing. My character? Jules Hamphert. What a great name for private eye - aloof, suave, catchy. I felt I'd created a name to match Agatha Christie's Hercule Poirot. Unfortunately, the story didn't match the character. I didn't realize that fact for several years. When I did, I changed the name and published the stories. But Jules Hamphert still holds a fragment of my heart and I have him in a story more appropriate to his discipline. Yes, it is still a mystery, but one that only Jules would lower himself to handle.

When writing Ancient Blood, my co-author agonized over the names, making sure they appropriately reflected the character, not only in culture, but also lifestyle. Yes, we created a history, a background life, for these characters since they will be repeated in the Ancient Blood series. We could have named our lead vampire "Ivan" which is a good Slavic name but "Ejup" added mystique and a hint of spice. As I originally wrote the first pass and being a typical Anglo-Saxon American, most of the names I used were very Anglicized. Jack Franklin, also an American, but living/working in Brazil, changed names to reflect the ambiance of the Amazon jungle. Queen Isa became Queen Itotia (eye-toe-chee-ya) and suddenly the story enshrouded itself in even more of the dark, forbidding, unknown Amazon jungle.

Minor characters also need to be named and appropriately. Don't cheat yourself, your readers or your character by tagging them with a wrong name. Imagine a Slavic priest with the name John Hanford? Step back. How about Bora Ianovic? How about a native Brazilian guide named Robert Sandini? Again, step back. How about Paulo Santos? Doesn't the second name bring a more vivid image to mind?

Now for those pesky characters who walk into the scene then disappear and well, maybe make one more appearance. Do you name them? That depends on what you want to do. You could name the butler, Hyde or - please don't - Jeeves. It adds a little atmosphere but really doesn't promote the story. Or have a name for your favorite diner waitress, Rita or Rose but it is not really necessary. So you can give a name to these ambiguous characters, like the butler who may be referred to several times but never really has a part in the tale. Don't dwell on too many trivial details about these characters. Remember, they are walk-on, walk-off. My friend calls these characters "pop ups" and seldom gives them a name. Telling the reader that Misty Roberts is wearing a camel-colored Chanel suit with pearl buttons is too much information. Especially if Misty's only reason to exist is to pass the note from Reggie to our heroine. Of course, you can give a little detail such as "Oh, here comes that snoopy neighbor's daughter." when Misty is spotted.

To keep things clear and focused, make up a chart or list of all the characters in your story, even the walk-ons. This will make sure you don't mis-queue somebody. I wrote a story with my lead's name as Mark, and then changed it to "Philip" and finally to "Noah." Imagine how confused I was during a read to stumble on Mark and Philip! I almost let it slip but decided to question just who these characters were. I checked my cast sheet and discovered my error.

To make naming a tad easier, use baby name books. I have one for boys and one for girls - and they are very old. Today I usually jump on the internet and search since I can specify boy names and also include race or culture. No reason to search through six thousand names when you can shorten the list to those of Native American, Greek, or Brazilian heritage. Happy naming...

Time Warping...

And it isn't even a science fiction tale! It is amazing what a writer can do when s/he takes the time to put pen to paper. Unfortunately, the writer can time warp the events and cause the reader to stumble, to drop out of the tale and wonder why it happened.

I wrote a segment. I re-read it repeatedly during my many edits and I even had it edited, professionally. The time warp was missed.

I happen to be reading it slowly and out loud for final edits. A great way to ascertain that the story actually sounds good, but another topic to be discussed another time.

I came to three small segments. I read segment one, it was good and I found no errors. I read segment two. Again, no errors. I started to read segment three and was at about the fourth paragraph when something niggled at me. It's not right.

Huh? So I re-read segment 2 and started to read segment 3 again. It "seemed" okay but still something bothered me. It was time to re-read all three segments.

BAM!

Segment one occurs on Wednesday night. Okay. Segment two occurs on Thursday morning. Okay. Segment three occurs on... Hmm? Reading the sentence, it would seem it was Monday morning. That can't be right. BUT, there it is - the offending line. It read ...Mr. Johnson wasn't smiling like he did every Monday morning... and today was supposedly Thursday. What's with Monday?

Exactly what was going on? Does Mr. Johnson only smile on Mondays? Rather than think about the possibilities and consequences, I deleted the word "Monday" from the text. Now the segment read just fine. For some reason I had time warped from Thursday morning back to or forward to a Monday morning. Not good.

One of my best writer friends shared her time warp experience. She, too, had edited the section several times and had professional editing done. (Guess this shows that even professionals are human, too!) Anyway, her female character, (names are being changed to protect my friend's WIP) Zooey was met by a cohort, Jack, at 2am. Now for the time warp aspect. Her brother had confirmed the assignment that afternoon.

He was speaking with Jack at 2am so Jack couldn't be with Zooey. Plus Zooey has a bad dream at 3am. Anyone who lives in a big city knows - you don't cross town in 20 minutes. So doing a job at 2am and being in REM sleep at 3am is practically impossible.

My friend is currently rewriting the original meeting with her brother as a working breakfast, conferring with Jack at 10pm and then Jack meeting Zooey at 2am. Zooey then has her dream the next night. So there is a lot of rewriting being done to eliminate time warping.

Sometimes a time warp is very subtle and only gets caught by a true aficionado of the subject. When did President Kennedy place the embargo (ban) on Cuba? When did Bay of Pigs happen? When was the missile crisis in Cuba? When did a man walk on the moon? Many other media events need to be accurately depicted. Mess up a date and somebody out there will nail you for it.

Another friend of mine wrote about a witch trial during the late 1700s in NW Ohio. Unfortunately, what she was describing happened in the New England locale since, at that particular time, NW Ohio was much more trapping adventures than pioneering. In fact, our community (yes, I live in NW Ohio) only had 40 homes in 1846. Again, a time warping fix to the rescue, the story was relocated to a New England area.

Therefore, when you write your tale of wonder, make sure that the incidents are plausible and in the proper time sequence. If your heroine is going to the ball at 8pm, don't have her digging with her fingers at 3pm in the garden, especially after having them manicured at 11am. Plus you don't take a frozen 24 pound turkey out of the freezer at 9am on Thanksgiving Day to serve to your guests at 2pm that afternoon. It just can't be done.

We all enjoy dancing the Time Warp (Rocky Horror Picture Show) and Captain Kirk can squeeze the spaceship Enterprise through a time warp, but your readers will shake their heads if you attempt a time warp in the story's facts.

Fragments

Parts of a sentence. Segments of usefulness. Catch phrases. A thought.

Your teachers hated them. Word processors despise them. And we writers love them. But are they useful?

First we ignore the rule - yes, that rule we learned back in school during English class. Every sentence must have a subject and a verb. It's a nice rule but does it always apply?

He looked up in the sky. What is it? A bird? A plane? No, it's Superman! Come to save the day!

Quick fragments blasting from the past to show us the way. "*A bird? A plane?*" and a longer last one. All are fragments and should have been expanded to "*Is it a bird? Is it a plane?* and *He has come to save the day!*" Now the sentence is no longer a fragment, it has a subject and a verb. All the English teachers are happy and content.

But, let's take a repeat of the corrected error...

He looked up in the sky. What is it? Is it a bird? Is it a plane? No, it's Superman! He has come to save the day!

Somehow, by making the sentence grammatically correct, it has lost its punch, its vitality. The impact of the moment is missing. Anticipation is missing.

This holds true for your writing. When composing a scene with action, use short, fragmented sentences to create and impart a sense of urgency. Long, drawn out descriptions and correct grammar slow down the reading.

Azbar's gold handled sword with the ruby encrusted hilt flashed through the air. It slashed the silken coverings of the pillow. His hand moved left, the sword's edge catching a glint of the lantern's light. The enemy twisted the green dagger in the low light, feinting right before lunging.

A very simple scene. Now, a little rewrite.

Azbar's sword flashed through the air. Feathers flew from a pillow. Left. Light glinted on the sword. A dagger twisted. The enemy feinted right before lunging.

Not the best examples, but... Basically the same scene. The 2nd attempt gave more imagery by making you see the movement quick and fast. I bet the feathers are still floating about in your mind which filled in the blanks. Do you really need to know the sword's handle was gold and the hilt was encrusted with rubies? Silk pillow? Cotton pillow? Does it matter if the dagger is green or maybe blue? Bottom line, a dagger twisted.

Fragments. Sentence mini-clusters can give more information than a long line of skillfully smithy-ed words. These fragments allow you, the writer, to convey images quickly to the reader.

Do you want -- *He jumped into the pristine, cold, fresh waters of the deep, azure-blue lake.*

Or do you want -- *He jumped into the lake. Cold. Fresh. Pristine. Deep.*

Remember, fragments can be your friends, especially if used properly and only when necessary.

WEEK 45:

Writer's Conference - A Marketing Tool

As you advance through your traditional marketing paces, you have a certain amount of control regarding some marketing aspects, along with minimal control over others. One of the marketing techniques that you have complete manageability over is the writer's conference.

When writer's conferences first began eons ago, their original intent was education. The writer or the writer-to-be would attend workshops with hopes of learning about the publishing world from other authors, agents, editors and publishers. This still holds true, but today there is so much more available to the attendee.

Taking part in a conference is your shot at marketing exactly how you want to be represented. What do I mean? You have the opportunity to market:

- Yourself
- Your book
- Your ideas
- A concept

Let's begin by discussing how to market yourself. When an agent or publisher makes the ever-important decision to represent your work, they're making this decision based on more than just words on paper. They're representing a human being. If you're someone who they feel will be difficult to work with, or who doesn't want to jump into the back-end of their writing project, you'll probably go nowhere. With this in mind, there are three main rules you should adhere to when attending a conference:

- be yourself,
- be yourself, and
- be yourself!

You MUST realize that your attitude, personality and opinions are your sales tools. To draw a crude comparison, when we find ourselves in the process of purchasing a new vehicle (not unlike getting a root canal), we're not only looking for a particular make and model (the product), but we're also looking for someone (the human aspect) who will make the whole experience a little easier to deal with. The same holds true in the publishing world.

When attending a writer's conference, you must mingle, meet people, and make friends and acquaintances. The publishing world, just like other "communities" such as dog training, or the disabled community, is fairly small. In one way or another, everybody knows everybody else. People carry a reputation with them. Create a bad reputation for yourself, and eventually everyone will know. Once this happens, it's almost impossible to change it. You need to relay the fact that as a writer, you're looking for a long-term relationship, not just a one-time business deal. If you are looking for the latter, maybe writing isn't right for you.

Let's now discuss the balance of what you need to market:

• your book,
• a concept, and
• an idea.

If you think about it, all three of these items can be considered as one.

If you're working on your initial proposal, or if you have two paragraphs left to complete your manuscript, you are NOT selling the artwork on the front or back cover, fancy graphs, or illustrations. You ARE selling a concept, solution or entertainment.

As a conference attendee, we will meander through multiple workshops, critique sessions, dinners, etc. The one main question that always surfaces as people get to know one another is, "What's your genre," or "What type of project are you working on?" Realize immediately that if you don't know the person you're talking with, you don't know if that individual is another writer, an agent or an editor. Don't bore them with, "Well, in chapter one... and in chapter two..." Your goal is to be able to describe your entire project in no more than two sentences. This is by far the most difficult task we as writers have to perform. How can we put years of work and research into two sentences? If you want to correctly represent your work, you'd better start learning now how to do this. While at conferences, I don't know how many times halfway through the event an editor would find me and say, "I heard from someone that you're working on 'abc' project."

Remember—we are representing a package. That package is our final deliverable product, and ourselves. One will not sell without the other.

Before attending your next conference, I recommend you sit down and make a list. This list should represent what you have to offer to the world. This should include items that list the positives, entertainment, self-help, etc. that your book offers-and you. Then, start editing. Delete adjectives, be-verb, adverbs, etc. Whittle your description down to the two sentences I described earlier. Just as the first paragraph of a book or article should be written and used as your "hook," so too must this short description. Once you complete your first draft, have it critiqued by your friends, and relatives. Get their honest opinion, and their first response. Use this data to go back to your drawing board (or computer) to polish what you've worked so hard to develop. THEN send it to a professional editor, word mangler, book doctor (whatever name you want to use) to give your work the finesse it deserves. Finally, memorize your two sentence description word-for-word. Best of luck, and enjoy the conference!

WEEK 46:

An Idea Generating Exercise

Sometimes your mind will go numb and you can't think of anything to write. You've called on your Muse but she (or he) just hasn't answered the request. You sit at your desk and struggle.

Step back! It is time to go on an adventure.

This will be a multi-step process so grab your trusty notepad and a writing instrument. Yes, this is going to a rustic adventure. You're actually going to write. So, with paper and pen in hand, take yourself to the local bookstore.

Step One: Pick any section of the bookstore with novels. Stay out of the do-it-yourself, how-to, and biography sections. Try the best-sellers, fantasy, romance, science fiction, horror, poetry or even young adult or children's sections.

Looking at the spine -- no cheating, no looking at any covers -- read the title of the book. Now, did it conjure up an image? Maybe even more? If so, write it down.

Make a list of maybe thirty or forty titles that caught your attention and gave you a taste of possibility.

Step Two: Move to another section of the bookstore. Select random books and read the first sentence of chapter one. Did it grab you? Better yet, did it suddenly expand your mind with a possible story line? If so, write it down. Again, do about fifty of these.

Step Three: Go home.

Step Four: Slowly go over the titles and opening lines you wrote down. Which ones make you laugh? Which ones make you see a vision? Which ones excite you? Try to analyze the why?

Step Five: Now, write some opening lines of your own. They don't have to be anything you're going to use but do put some thought into them. Sit back and evaluate your line against those you wrote down from the bookstore. Which is better? And why?

Step Six: Take one of the best of your lines you wrote and see if you can expand on it. Give it a full paragraph. Push the boundary and go for a full page. Is the image 'clicking' and can you expound to either make it a story or perhaps chapter 1 of a novel?

Step Seven: Place the lists you created in a safe location where you can easily put your fingers on them at a later date. Allow a few days, weeks or even months to pass then pull the lists out and repeat steps four through six. This time, check to see if the lines match your previous thoughts. What is funny? Which one makes you see more than just a quick thought?

Doing this exercise will wake up the Muse in you and get the juices flowing.

I read just the first paragraph (4 lines) of a novel about a Viking. Between the title and that paragraph, I was able to expand and begin a new work-in-progress. The imagery was amazing and exploded in my mind as I wrote my first sentence. I continued with the paragraph and then wrote the complete outline for the novel which I may or may not use for this year's NaNoWriMo. Uh, in all honesty, I was given a great idea for another novel which I have outlined. These ideas have been saved to a directory where I already have a couple of other outlines for future projects. I know this exercise works.

WEEK 47:

Flashbacks

I read this someplace and truly wish I could remember where: "*A good rule of thumb for characters is simple—if they can't stand on their own without a backstory, then develop them more as a person.*"

Truer words have never been spoken. Perhaps it was my mentor who told me that when I started writing.

Backstory should *facilitate* your character, not *define* your character. Backstory is sugar in the cake. What your character does during the story is the cake.

Forget the brooding, tortured soul. It's an overused and oh-so-familiar archetype so many people are annoyed with for that very reason. The only thing defining the character is their past. They don't do anything of value in the story. They sit there and brood, re-hashing the past to the reader with their backstory. Unfortunately, this is NOT the character to have.

A character can definitely have a tortured past, but they also have to do something substantial during the story. Many writers seem to think giving a character "a past full of dark secrets" will make them interesting. Many readers find this mega-dark secrets thing... well, boring. Think about it. Doesn't it seem logical it would be more interesting for the character to generate those dark secrets during the story process?

Let's analyze why this dark secret/tortured past scenario is so boring. What is the most common way for people to get across this past to the reader? They use: a) Flashbacks or b) The character bluntly tells us what happened to them. Listen. *Boring!*

Flashbacks

Flashbacks are not effective at holding our attention because it slows the forward momentum of the story by going back to rehash the past. As a reader, we don't want to stop that momentum. We want to keep going forward. Flashbacks don't progress the story other than providing trivial or, sometimes, vital information. There's no action associated with a flashback since it moves the reader to another period of time in the past, rather than forward.

The character bluntly tells us what happened to them.

Talk about *telling* rather than *showing*! By doing that, it automatically is dull, flat and boring. Period.

You can definitely use flashbacks of the backstory, but attempt to keep it to a minimum. Every character has a backstory, so don't think this means you need to leave out a character's backstory. A cake without sugar would be tasteless. Also, a cake with too much sugar would be sickeningly sweet—you need to find that happy medium of how much backstory is needed. Remember, it will be different for each story and each character.

Backstories can be the vehicle to show your character's motive. How? The most important thing to making an interesting character is for them to participate in the action of the story, to move forward with a motive. All characters have a history. If a character's parents were killed, have the character take action to actively find the killer and enact revenge. Even better, have the character help someone else who experienced the same thing. If the character has made mistakes in the past, that's fine. Let the character make amends to fix those mistakes.

Backstories are a double-edged sword. It is your job to hone it properly without slicing up the story.

Evil Villains

Exactly how often does your villain raise his hands near his face and rub them while casting a maniacal gaze to the left or right? S/He then lets out an evil "mwah-ha-ha!" followed by "My devious plot is about to unfold!" Really! I'm asking, how many times?

In reality, even my title is redundant. How many times have you stumbled onto a good villain?

Let's step back and evaluate this stereotypical character—the villain. They exist to confound the protagonist, the hero(ine).

Never once does an antagonist think they are evil or bad. They consider themselves, for the most part, just like everyone else. They exist to have what they want. The catch is simple—they're not supposed to have it. THAT is what makes them a villain.

Take the "evil" queen in Snow White. For my purposes, we'll use the children's fairy tale. Sure, she dabbled in the black arts and wanted Snow White killed. But, in her defense, it was only to get rid of the competition. Yes, a little drastic, but the queen only saw Snow White as somebody who was about to usurp her position as the most beautiful in the kingdom. You tell me, what beauty queen wouldn't kill to keep the title?

But, I digress. Never once did the evil queen think of herself as bad, the villain or even evil.

In your next work, think about the antagonist in a different light. Don't attempt to describe your villain as evil incarnate, or so vile that black paled beside him/her.

With that said, there are times when evil is just plain bad. Demons, Satan and such creatures. But, even Satan doesn't think of himself as evil. In fact, according to stories, he warred with God to take control. Who hasn't done that? In today's world we have winners and losers. That's just the way it is. Satan lost but I don't think he ever really saw himself as a bad person. Even when Satan lured Eve with the apple, he was trying to help her to see things as God saw them. Yeah, it was a con job.

There are those "creatures" who perform bad deeds. Yes, you could consider them evil. They probably don't see themselves as bad but just getting the job done. Just like thugs who crack kneecaps for a living—it's all in a day's work. Yes, they probably know it's not the proper thing to do but they have a job to perform.

Consider this. If an entity is born out of the clouds of heaven, is s/he immediately considered good? Do angels sing at every footstep of this entity? Do they go around stating how wonderful, good, perfect they are? The same applies to the entity spawned out of the depths of hell. That entity doesn't trudge around stating how bad they are. Do they rub their hands in a ball and let out a maniacal laugh? Maybe they do but that's part of the stereotypical job description YOU'VE given them.

In the future, never have your villain think they are the vilest creature or they are performing the evilest deed. They're just average Joe doing what they need to do—confounding the hero(ine). Even the good guys, the hero(ine)s do bad things, so a villain is just doing bad things with better flair. SHOW how evil they are, don't bother telling us with fancy descriptive words like "vile," "evil," "bad," "disgusting," "wicked," "malevolent," "despicable," "abominable," or "malicious." As they say—Action speaks louder than words. SHOW us the action. Show us the villain.

⁂

The World According To...

I asked a writer friend what type of world he was creating for his tale. His reply: A medieval monarchy.

Hmm? At first thought I saw a castle, ladies-in-waiting, knights, grand feasts, jousting and peasants.

Was I ever wrong! He explained there was a queen who ruled the country. Her throne was carved from a mountainside with a stone wall to protect it. She had a lieutenant who controlled the army of three hundred warrior men. Her people worked the fields and owned nothing. The warriors were unmarried and lived only to serve their queen. Ah, yeah, right.

To me, it was a bleak world with too many conundrums that vexed my puny mind to see his vision. The way I saw it—If I were a warrior, there'd be a few more desires than just wanting to serve the queen. Like *what's in it for me*? Plus, the people of the kingdom loved to work the fields and have nothing. Even the slaves in America's South had a building they got to call home.

So let's look at world building using government as the basis. Every government has a leader. In this case, the queen, which makes it a monarchy. There is a pecking order in any monarchy once you drop below the level of immediate royalty: king, queen, princes and princesses. That would be something like Grand Duke, Archduke, Duke, Earl or Count, Baron, Knight, Esquire or Gentleman and finally the peasant. There are a few sub-divisions of the before listed group, but it is a nice general list. The bottom line is simple—These are the lords and ladies of the court until you hit peasant level.

Again, to say you have a monarchy world would indicate many things beyond just the government. The military becomes part of the equation. The lords would have military to offer to the royals for service. This would be in addition to the royal's own military. Since there is military, they are not going to serve for the pleasure of being able to serve. Now the world building gets a little more complicated. Finances come into play. Again, each "lord" would pay up to the next higher person and each higher person would "share the wealth" down to the next level. In other words, the peasant would pay a tax to his lord and that lord would pay to his lord. This would continue until the royal at the top ultimately received what was due. In return, favors and finances were shared back down the line with the peasant getting the smallest cut—if there was any available by then.

Following finances comes Commerce. Peasants may work the earth but somebody has to sell THIS HARVEST. This commerce may be totally enclosed within the kingdom or it may be more involved and include rivalry kingdoms and/or cities.

As you can see, there is definitely more to creating a world than just stating that a queen sits on a stone throne on a mountainside. If you follow Commerce, it will lead to Territories (including landscape), Seasons, Environment, Health and the list continues including Religion, Entertainment and Hobbies.

Right now I see a queen sitting on a stone throne wondering what the hell happened!

⁇

Writing A Series

When I'm at a writing conference, or in a chatroom or visiting a writing group, I find it amazing how many questions I receive about writing a series. *Exactly how does one go about writing a series? What secrets are there to the genre? Do you write one long story and cut it up into sections?* And the list goes on.

First and foremost – all series are genre-less. It isn't a genre but a collection of books within a genre – be it romance, western, fantasy, science fiction, non-fiction, horror or whatever. I can probably name at least one series in almost any specific genre. Western: Zane Grey's "Trilogy" consisting of *Betty Zane, The Last Trail*, and *The Spirit of the Border*. Science Fiction? Orson Scott Card's "Ender's Shadow" Series with *Ender's Shadow, Shadow of the Hegemon, Shadow Puppets* and *Shadow of the Giant*. I can even get a little more specific with a tighter genre that includes two sub-categories. How about Amish Historical Romance? Murray Pura's "Snapshots in History" which includes *The Wings of Morning, The Face of Heaven* and *Whispers Of A New Dawn*.

My friend, Elyse Salpeter just released book 2 of her "The Children of Demilee" series. The first book is *The World of Karov*. Her new book is *The Ruby Amulet*. What genre is this series? Offhand I'd call it fantasy, YA with a touch of darkness. Check it out at Amazon.com for the ebook version. It is also available in paperback.

I currently have a co-author (Jack Franklin) for a series and our first book of "The Vamazonian Chronicles" is available with the title of *Ancient Blood: The Amazon*. It is available at Amazon.com in both paperback and ebook versions. It is also available at B&N, Damnation Books and your local bookstores. It is the first in a planned six book series that has been outlined. Book 2 (*Ancient Blood: The Homeland*) is currently undergoing final edits.

Second. There are two approaches to a series. You can write one long epic tale (think Lord of the Rings) where it is broken at a point that satisfies but also leaves the reader wanting more. The other method is to write a complete story in one book but have a thread that will continue into the next book and the one after that. Actually, Lord of the Rings has a thread working through all three books but the difference is – a reader can't pick up book 2 (The Two Towers) and finish it and be contented. The reader needs to know the beginning and find a conclusion.

In our Vamazonian Chronicles, each novel is a complete tale but the continuing thread gets addressed but not resolved. It is possible for a reader to pick up any of the books and have a satisfying tale with an ending. The underlying thread is not answered but the story is done until the next book.

Sometimes the series is even simpler. It is a group of books, each a complete story, with one main character or locale. Series needn't be long tales. I read a book of three short stories. Each story took place in the same house. The stories involved the original owner, another set of owners and finally, the current owner. I found the stories a delight to read and also how easily the author had woven the tales together, linking each new story back to the previous tales. Sometimes a series can be recognized by the title alone such as those written by Denise Vitola: *Opalite Moon, Quantum Moon*, and *Manjinn Moon*.

As noted earlier, series can be written by a single author, co-written by two authors, or even a collection of three or more authors.

To make it very simple. Series are just books which most people find easier to read in the sequence in which they are written. There's really no secret or mystery behind a series. It is just the ability to tell a continuing tale while not boring the reader.

☐

Character Details

Rodney walked into the room. He was tall, dark-haired, wearing a blue shirt and black slacks. The gold ring on his right hand glistened with a diamond. His blue eyes glanced about. Victoria liked what she saw.

Wasn't that an exciting description? How many writers will scribe those sentences to reveal a character. I would call that every newbie's fatal first mistake. Some may even give a more detailed report with—

Rodney walked into the room. His blue eyes scanned the room. Standing over six foot, his dark-brown wavy brown hair was impeccably combed. The blue shirt was tight and revealed his rippling muscles. The black jeans were Western cut and fit like a glove. He wore custom cowboy boots. A diamond glittered in the gold ring on his right hand. Victoria smiled, she liked what she saw.

Another attempt at a feeble blow-by-blow description. Why not make the descriptive detail a part of the story rather than a boring itemized list?

Rodney strolled into the room, his piercing ice-blue eyes locating the bar. Victoria noticed him immediately since he stood above the others in the crowd. Party revelers parted as he made his way toward his goal, the bar, where Victoria perched on a nearby stool. She couldn't help noticing the blue shirt, the top two buttons undone to reveal the rippling tanned muscles. The silver buckle swayed with each swagger, mesmerizing her. The tight, black jeans hugged his hips and legs down to the custom cowboy boots with the silver toe tips and heel guards. Her breath caught—Was that a diamond wedding band? Victoria exhuled with relief. It was the right hand and the ring was just a diamond ring. Victoria glanced once more at the total package walking toward her. She smiled, he'd made his entrance and now it was her turn.

By using another character to reveal the details, the reader can get a better understanding of the two characters. Above, Rodney has a swagger, is definitely proud of his physique and wants people to notice him. They do, they separate like the Red Sea before him as he moves through the crowd. At the same time, Victoria is letting us see him in her eyes and how he affects her and how she has already decided that she is on the hunt and found her quarry.

Surprisingly, locales are characters, too. A reader hates to peruse the travelogue blurb about the scenery, to wit:

Grace peered out the window at the snow-capped mountains of the Rockies. The highway was busy as the truck went up the slope toward the ski lodge. It was summer and the crystal-clear blue waters of the lake reflected the distant mountains.

Now wasn't that just exciting?

Grace jammed the clutch down and shifted into a lower gear as the truck slowly churned its way up the highway toward the ski lodge. She didn't have time to enjoy the beauty of the snow-capped mountain tops nor the breath-taking view of the crystal-clear blue lake just over the edge. Grace exhaled slowly, very glad it was summer and she didn't have to also fight snow, ice and wintry blasts to keep the truck moving forward. Her eyes flicked to the lake and for a mere second, enjoyed the mirrored distant mountains.

Again, using a character to give us the details involves us in the story. Consider the positive side to this method: Upped word count. Did you notice that the final version usually involved more words. It isn't fluffing the story by any means. A good writer involves the reader. If the reader wanted a grocery list of details, there are other avenues for that potential. I call it an outline.

When I outline my character, I use short details—almost like the very first paragraph which would have read: *Name-Rodney, 6 ft tall, blue eyes, dark-brown hair, blue shirt, black jeans, cowboy boots, diamond ring. Struts and swaggers when walking.* Almost reads like the first paragraph.

Give the reader the details but impart them in a subtle method. Like we are constantly being told: Show, don't tell.

WEEK 52:

Reading and Writing La-La Land

Have you ever read a book and got to a point where you stop, look up and frown? At the same time, deep inside your mind you hear the words "*What the hell was that?*"

Your reader was jolted out of the world you'd created and now had a choice - (a) shrug the shoulders and try to get back to the warm, cozy spot they were in OR (b) put the book down.

More than likely, depending on the jolt and what might have to be done - the option most often picked will be "B" and you, the writer, don't want that!

As a writer, you are creating a haven for your reader. It is a place where they can escape and be entertained, forgetting the worries of what needs to be done. A reader will flip pages, oblivious to the world about them until one of a few options happen:

- An alarm goes off telling them they need to stop
- Somebody interrupts them for a meal or do work
- The munchies and drinks are empty and the stomach calls
- It gets dark and they need to turn on a light
- A slow scene or end of chapter with no carry-over to next chapter
- Jolted out of the story

You can only control the last two options and the very last option is one you DON'T want to happen - EVER!

You may be asking what I mean by jolting the reader out of the story. Let me give you a couple of examples, some are so subtle that even the best can be tripped up.

Example 1: *It was high noon in the Nation's Capital as she dashed into Union Station. She strutted across the Main Hall, her heels clicking loudly on the linoleum floor. She gazed upward at the hideous gargoyles decorating the perimeter of the ceiling.*

Example 2: *He held his position, waiting, watching. Texas was a gunslinger's heaven. Behind one of those huge saguaro cacti he knew Bill Cassidy was hiding, waiting for him to make a mistake.*

Example 3: *Daisy stretched as she awoke and then smiled as she gazed out on her first morning in California. The Pacific Ocean shimmered as she watched the distant sunrise shed the clouds and ripple across the incoming waves.*

Each of the above could have jolted your reader out of the story and made them question your writing expertise. I worked outside of Union Station and rode the train every day to and from work. Never once did I see any linoleum in Union Station. All the floors were marble or carpet in some of the nicer stores and restaurants that didn't want marble. But they didn't have linoleum. Also, I don't remember seeing any hideous gargoyles. They do have some faces and statues, but I would hardly call them hideous. I've traveled a lot in my life and been to Texas many times and love the cacti but again, the saguaro cactus is only native to the Sonoran Desert area which is basically in Arizona. Finally, I've yet to see a sunrise come out of the Pacific Ocean while visiting California. I've seen a sunrise in Hawaii, but then again, I was a lot further west. If you stand on the Californian shore, facing the Pacific Ocean, 99.44% of the time, I'm willing to bet the sunrise will be to your back.

Those were subtle but very obvious errors made by writers in stories I have read and/or edited. There are many other simple mistakes many writers make. Blood is pumped out of the body when shot and/or stabbed. It does not spread out like a seeping balloon. Horses can gallop fast but not all day. Think Pony Express. At full speed, a horse can go about 10 miles and then it will need to rest. Also, remember the rider is going to suffer during the outburst of a full gallop.

Today's television and movie drama has caused writers to lose sight of reality. A thrown knife will flip through the air so at that moment, there is a 50/50 chance of the blade striking the object. If that object is a human, the accuracy of catching the open area between the rib cage is even finer and hitting the heart, really pushes the odds limit.

By the way, there is more to flashing a sword around in a battle. I know because I took a couple of hours of sword practice with a person who does professional sword fighting at Renaissance Fairs. Until that moment, my story lacked authenticity during the battle scenes.

A simple fact can trip you, the writer, up. A simple misfact can jolt your reader out of your story. Be sure, never guess.

BONUS WEEK:

War and Sex

Do you know how to write a good war scene? A great sex scene? Better question - Do you need to write a war or sex scene?

First a little history. Years ago I belonged to a small writing group in Washington, DC. I was having the group critique a novel I was working on, feeding them no more than 30 pages each month. Finally, one member of the group was bold enough to tell me either to allow my characters to get it on and make out or drop that story line but she was tired of all the teasing. The dam had a leak and suddenly it was broken. Another member jumped on the band-wagon to inform me either have a battle or not have one but don't lead up to a battle only to let it fizzle out.

In other words, I had two story lines which my readers weren't enjoying. One was the to-be intimate romance between my lead characters. The other was a major battle. So, taking the bull by the horns, I attacked the battle issue and let it begin but to avoid any major descriptions, I sent my lead character to another dimension. The sex, well, I was reluctant to have any erotica in my fantasy but I still wanted that sexual tension. It was an issue but I was able to find a happy mixture.

Until my paid editor ripped it apart. The battle scene was a cop-out. My editor told me bluntly - either remove the battle option from the book or write the damned thing. Don't send your character to another dimension to avoid the battle. Strangely, she was okay with the sex aspect and thought I'd held the interest while keeping the story line moving but it still could use a little more 'ompf' to make it stronger.

To get the battle scene proper I imposed on a friend to give me some sword fighting lessons. Needless to say, we had to do this outside where the whole world could watch me do - his words, not mine - the monkey dance. We used bamboo swords for my protection until I got the hang of it. My one son filmed it but that was a futile effort since he was laughing so hard the camera he held jiggled all around. The neighborhood group of boys stood in the cul-de-sac and watched Mr. Nailor do his yip-yowl monkey dance. When I had finally gotten my steps learned, we moved to real metal swords and I finally knew what it meant to feel the grip in my hand, to relish the ring of metal as the swords came together and one would slide down the other. It was exhilarating. I learned how to write a sword-fighting scene and hence, a battle scene. Still, I didn't know exactly how it would feel to impale a person. Unfortunately, I wouldn't —

or should I say fortunately I didn't need that experience. An undertaker friend explained to me how it would feel and the difficulty. To say the blade pierced like a hot knife into butter is not totally accurate.

As to the sex. I was on my own, for the most part, since my wife was adamant I couldn't hire somebody. I had to go with my gut and what I knew.

But the truth was, either my character had to stay and play or I had to eliminate the story line of intimate sex. A reader will only go along with the tease a few times before putting the book down. This doesn't mean you need to go 'all out' and have an explicit sex manual. As I told my friend a few days ago when we were discussing writing sex:

Studs know how to be sexy because they have conquered. Sensual women know how to lure because they have seduced successfully. A virgin can only know so much and then she is no longer a virgin but a scared little girl who now knows the truth. Your heroine can vamp just so far before it is out of her realm of expertise. Think of it as a innocent girl who performs her first lap dance. She can do the moves and be sexy. She can grind on the man. But, at some point, she is going to be surprised when the man becomes aroused. She will probably stop her first lap dance. On her 2nd or 3rd lap dance she will continue until the man reaches the point of no return and again, she is going to be surprised. AT THAT POINT, the innocent girl is no longer innocent. She might still be a virgin but only technically. She is now a woman of the world with only the actual act to complete the full transformation.

A writer doesn't have to give every detail of the love-making act. There is an art to writing a sex scene that will appease the reader. Remember that first move for a boy from his hand on her shoulder to awkwardly fumbling against her breast? It is sex that every reader can identify with and that is what you want. You don't need to describe bedroom acrobatics to satisfy the reader unless you are writing extreme erotica or porn where it is expected. My friend, Mitch Whitington, wrote a fantastic article on how to write sex as 'afterglow' which really defines the moment. You can find that earlier in this book.

Also, here's some tidbits to build up your arsenal of how to write war and sex. Use the proper word. A battle scene is not an engagement. The combatants are not a love-struck couple going ga-ga over a ring. It is a bloody, brutal and vicious event. It is not to be glorified. Death is final. As for sex, there are many synonyms for the sexual organs but as one writer told me at a symposium, call it what it is if you're going to call it anything. Also, avoid all the colorful adjectives. As he said - throbbing and juicy are heavily over-used. Or as the chaplain so aptly told us when I first joined the Navy and was going through boot camp: Most of you young men are eighteen or older. You no longer go wee-wee or poo-poo so quit giggling like a 16-year-old virgin girl when somebody uses what you think to be a cuss-word. Body functions and the Vietnam War are real.

So, to paraphrase that colorful chaplain: War and sex are real. Write it real.

Appendix

Appendix (Continued)

Appendix (Continued)

ABOUT THE AUTHOR

My name is Robert S. Nailor but most people just call me Bob.

I'm retired from the federal government. I was a computer geek and still do some programming yet today. One would think I should have plenty of time to write but I actually seem to have less now. So, I try to force myself to sit down and write, but that doesn't always work. Today, writing is fun and I find it relaxing. I get to visit those fantastic and strange places within my mind and well, if I don't come back right away, there is no longer somebody behind me writing on a pink slip of paper.

I live with my wife, Violet, in a ranch home snuggled into a small wooded acre in NW Ohio. I moved to Ohio in 1953. I have four sons and currently have eight grandchildren - 6 granddaughters and 2 grandsons.

My interests are travel (have RV, will travel), gardening, music, cooking and reading. So where do I travel? I've been in 46 of the 50 states and strangely, Hawaii is one of the states I've visited. I have also visited two of our territories - Puerto Rico and Virgin Islands and been through the Panama Canal. Traveling allows me to add the ambiance to my stories and to some of the characters, also. Gardening for me is a bit gamey since we live in the country and have the wildlife visiting us constantly -- deer, rabbits, raccoons, birds, squirrels and many other creatures. So vegetables don't always make it to harvest but what does is more than tasty. There are flowers, sometimes too many, to keep me busy. Music? I love New Age music and my favorite group is Mannheim Steamroller... and not just because of their fabulous Christmas albums; I was hooked on them before that. I also have created some of my own electronic music which I've been told is pretty good. Should I mention cooking? I love to cook and do gourmet cooking. Having worked with Boy Scouts for several years, I have taught many boys the basics of cooking beyond hotdogs and beans. I have won quite a few contests. As to what I read; well obviously a lot of science fiction and fantasy although horror, romance, adventure and other genres are also great reads when they catch my attention.

Visit me at http://www.bobnailor.com

OTHER WORKS BY THE AUTHOR

NOVELS

Pangaea: Eden Lost ~ a Barclay Havens, relic hunter misadventure
     http://www.amazon.com/dp/B00JH8MKMM/
Ancient Blood: The Amazon ~ a new vampire series
     http://www.amazon.com/dp/B0093CKYUW
Three Steps: The Journeys of Ayrold ~ an Irish tale with the Little People
     http://www.amazon.com/dp/B005MZS89I/
2012 Timeline Apocalypse ~ When the Mayan calendar comes to an end
     http://www.amazon.com/dp/B005VGO3VU

ANTHOLOGIES

    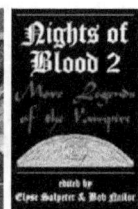 

Telling Tales of Terror ~ essays on how to write horror and dark fiction
Mother Goose Is Dead ~ a collection of fracture fairy tales
Dead Set: A Zombie Anthology ~ a collection of unusual zombie tales
The Complete Guide to Writing Paranormal-Vol 1 ~ various subjects
Nights of Blood 2 ~ various takes on the vampire, a great collection
Guide to Writing Science Fiction ~ essays on how to write science fiction

PLUS MORE at Bob Nailor's Author Web: http://www.bobnailor.com

SAMPLE READ of PANGAEA: EDEN LOST

Chapter One ~ THE INTERVIEW

She sat behind the massive cherry wood desk, covertly keeping tabs on me, smiling, knowing she was the almighty guardian who protected those on the other side of the highly polished mahogany double doors. Strangely, I felt I knew the individuals I could not see. They were considering me to retrieve some archeological artifact for them. Others had requested the same services with the only differences being the sought-after object and the location of the meeting. My hearing is uncanny. The conversation on the other side sounded like whispered secrets, eavesdropping, while others who might sit near me would never hear a thing. With only the guardian, I sat alone in the over-bearing and huge chamber. The sound of the secretary's pen scratching across the surface of the paper annoyed me because she seemed to be writing the same 47thing repetitively — angled stroke up, angled stroke down, angled stroke up, angled stroke down with a curl at end, lift pen, small move, small stroke up, double curled down stroke with a quick short upstroke followed by a sweeping down curve and a very short horizontal exit line with an upward curve and then a period. The diamond ring on her hand glistened. I smiled. She was writing her soon-to-be married name: *Mrs. John...*

I heard the conversation on the other side of the door coming to an end. It was time. A distinct *'we are in agreement, gentlemen?'* let me know I would be called into the next room, behind those massive doors Mrs. John Tedo-something considered her obligation to guard.

The buzzer sounded and the secretary glanced at me with the faintest of frowns on her face as I stood in preparation. "They're ready for you, Dr. Havens," she said. "You may go in." She casually waved her arm in the direction of the majestic nine-panel mahogany doors.

My feet padded softly on the heavy dark green carpeting and across the two colorful Persian rugs. I tripped momentarily on the second rug as I made my way toward the room. I paused briefly before those sacred, highly polished doors of the hallowed university's board of directors and took a long, deep breath. My hand gripped the brightly polished brass handle, and I slowly started to exhale. I was definitely stalling.

"I said you may go in, Dr. Havens," Mrs. John-whatever repeated. The timber of her voice clearly indicated she was a bit miffed that I wasn't following her instructions.

I ran a finger around my shirt's collar, pulling at it before I pushed the door open and entered. A moment's hesitation before strolling in allowed me to garner a bit of strategy and information. A long wooden conference table commanded the center of the room. On the opposite side of the table from me were five very stodgy-appearing men of various ages, wearing suits of different shades, running from dark gray or black to deeper colors of blue. They appraised me as I did them. A quick reconnaissance of the room as I strode forward revealed three more people, two men and a woman, who sat near the doors I had come through. The two gentlemen sat beside each other and were near my age, both were dressed in almost identical dark blue suits. One had light brown hair while the gentleman in the middle was dark-haired. The woman sat on the right side of the dark-haired man and she was perhaps a year or two younger, wore a floral dress which, in my opinion, didn't strike me as her style. The doors silently closed, and with a click, the room was now secured. A huge tapestry hung on one wall and portraits, not pictures, of whom I was sure were prior trustees, adorned the mahogany paneled walls. The lighted, multi-tiered and definitely over indulgent crystal chandelier above us seemed useless against the strong sunlight streaming through the four tall, beveled, lead glass windows.

"Ah, Dr. Havens." The gentleman seated in the middle of the five pushed on the table to assist his standing. He was slender, short, with thinning salt and pepper hair and I guessed probably in his late sixties. It was his dark, deep set eyes that grabbed my attention as he leaned across the highly polished table. There was fire in them. He offered his hand to shake. "I'm Dr. Peter Vanderguud, Trustee and president of this esteemed board."

I locked hands, surprised by the fact he had a firm grip which belied the frail appearance.

"Let me introduce the others starting with Dr. Trent Hall on my extreme right at the end. Next to me is Dr. Edgar Baxter."

My eyes kept going to Hall, a younger gentleman who appeared to be very near my age. He seemed familiar, yet I couldn't place him and the name hadn't tripped any correlative memory triggers with the man. My mind wandered, hearing some of the names and I quickly realized I now had no idea who was who other than Hall and Vanderguud. The guy next to Hall, was his name Baxter or Jasper? I could tell I was going to make a less than perfect impression on this distinguished group.

"Do you have any idea why we have requested your services?" Vanderguud asked as he took his seat.

"Not exactly," I replied, standing in front of the table. "But I'd hazard a guess you want a relic retrieved."

There was a heavy sigh from the end of the table where Hall sat as he fiddled with a pen, tapping it to the notepad, letting his index finger and thumb slide down the length of the pen's barrel, lift it into the air, watch the pen flip over, to repeat once more with another irritating tap.

"We need you to find—" Vanderguud paused, pursed his lips and closed his eyes in thought. His left index finger nervously tapped the tightened lower lip. His eyes opened and he gazed at me. "Ah... hmm... yes. Not a relic but a certain relic's location." He smiled. "I am hoping that is the best way to phrase our request." He casually cocked his head to the right.

"That's what I do," I replied. I hated games and it seemed we had one in progress. I'm a for-hire relic hunter. You pay me and I go get what you want, no matter where. Why the damned delay? Then his words hit me. *A relic's location?*

"Oh, enough," Hall blurted. "Here."

A large object twisted and spun in the air on a trajectory toward me. I grabbed, fumbled, and jostled it around in my hands before dropping it onto my boot to finally wobble a few inches beyond my feet. I bent down to pick it up. At least it hadn't broken and I sighed quietly in relief.

"My God, Peter!" Hall yelled and glared at Vanderguud. "Surely you're not going to allow this clumsy buffoon to be involved with something as valuable as this." He threw his hands into the air with disgust.

"Trenton," Vanderguud shouted and raised his hand to silence the man.

My mind raced. Suddenly I recognized the name. Trent hadn't connected, but the name Trenton did.

"Fine," Hall snarled at Vanderguud and turned his irritation at me. "Okay, Barky, you've got the stone. What is it?" His voice literally oozed in rudeness and it was that sneering of the words which reinforced the recognition of the voice. The past came alive.

"Two-Ton?" I blurted and stared at Hall. "Two-Ton Tren-Ton?" Could this be the man I'd attended university with during my freshman year? The pain-in-the-ass snit I had been forced to share a dorm room with for a whole miserable year?

There was a small choked snicker from the back of the room. It was the woman.

"I prefer Dr. Trenton Hall." He glared at me with narrowed eyes. His actions and words belied his emotions—the white knuckles revealed his tension by how tightly he now held the pen between his two fisted hands.

"As you wish, Trent. Just remember, my name is Dr. Barclay Havens." I paused and glanced at the other men before once more looking at Hall. "I see you've lost a few pounds since we last met." *I would guess maybe two hundred pounds.*

"So, Dr. Havens." Trenton once more took charge. "Exactly what do you think you have in your possession? Please demonstrate your expertise, those uncanny skills we've heard so much about." He waved his hand in the air with a flourish and wiggled his fingers. "Oh, do enlighten us with all your mystic learning."

I rolled the large stone around in my hands and couldn't help but notice the indent. The rock was obviously a form of granite with what appeared to be small lava inclusions, which was a bit different. The focal point was the indentation: smooth, partial circular shape with a definite flat end. It reminded me of what a chunk of clay would look like if you shoved the bottom half of a thermos or a large Pringles can part way into it. This was definitely an enigma.

"We're waiting," Trenton said. A smirk curled the edges of his lips.

"My first inclination is granite regarding the rock itself. Now about this indentation—obviously manmade and I wouldn't hesitate to say probably by a metallic cylinder. Of course, I'm willing to guess this is something you already know." I cocked an eyebrow at Trenton. "Right?" The smug, smirking smile dissipated as the muscles about his lips contorted and jerked.

136

"Gentlemen!" Vanderguud glared at Hall. "Before we start another pissing match, Dr. Havens, would you be so kind as to hand me the rock?"

I stepped to the conference table and gently placed the stone in front of Vanderguud. I tried not to smile at his calling our little banter a pissing match.

"Now, Trenton," Vanderguud said. "Please *hand* Dr. Havens the cylinder." He again glared at the younger man. "Hand it to him." Vanderguud spoke the words slowly and distinctly.

I watched Trenton roll his eyes and grimace, he was totally pissed. He reached below the table's top, into his lap or beside him then held up a bright metallic cylinder for me to see.

I moved to Trenton, leaned over and carefully retrieved the object from his hand.

"You're in way over your head, Barky," Trenton whispered and offered that grin I despised from our school days.

"Maybe yes, maybe no," I replied, noting he still wore the same cheap aftershave from years past. Some things never change it seems." I wrinkled my nose.

"Now, Dr. Havens." Vanderguud reached out to the granite piece. "As you have already mentioned, the object you now hold was extracted from this stone." His hand patted the granite chunk.

I studied the piece. It had to be a relic even if it didn't make sense. The stone was old, possibly millions of years, yet this metallic cylinder was of the finest craftsmanship: highly honed, mirror polished and nearly perfect. There was no rust, no dents, and no indication of the slightest scratch. There was nothing except the shiny tube.

"Well?" Trenton quipped.

I held it to my ear and gently shook the tube. A soft rustle could be heard. Something was inside. Yet there didn't appear to be any visible means of opening the object. Using a trick I'd learned in the Himalayan monastery under Master Jampa Rabten Lobsang, I softly played my fingers over the surface hoping any possible seam would be felt.

"What the hell are you doing?" Trenton asked. His hand reached out to wrest the cylinder from me. I pulled back, clutching the prize closer.

Vanderguud politely held out his hand. "Dr. Havens, allow me."

His smile was hypnotic and I handed him the coveted possession.

"Your verdict?" Vanderguud asked.

I eyed the group of men opposite me. This was the challenge, the test of make or break. I reached deep inside and used my well of resources as I'd been taught and quickly gleaned and processed the collected data.

"As we all can tell," I started. "It definitely came from that particular piece of stone which of course makes the situation even more problematic. How can something so new be a part of something as old as Earth itself? Although I didn't find a seam, I am guessing there is something soft, perhaps a manuscript or parchment inside. Has anybody been able to ascertain the exact composition of the cylinder?"

Vanderguud adjusted his glasses. "Very good questions and answers, Dr. Havens."

"I had the item x-rayed," the gentlemen to Vanderguud's immediate left offered. "Dr. Horace Allister is the name."

I hadn't thought my expression was that of being lost or confused but it was kind of Allister to offer his name since I hadn't remembered it.

"What did the x-ray reveal?" I asked and nonchalantly looked about me. If they weren't going to offer me a chair, I was going to find one myself.

"Trenton!" Vanderguud motioned. "Get Dr. Havens a chair. Wherever are our manners?"

I watched Trenton recoil at the thought of doing manual labor.

"Here." The young man with the light brown hair who sat at the back of the room came forward with a folding chair. "Will this be adequate?"

"Thanks. I don't need luxury," I replied. "Just a place to park my butt." I sat and quickly turned my attention back to Allister. "I'm sorry. You were saying?"

"We attempted x-rays," Allister said. "It defied our exams and tests."

"Tests?" I questioned.

"Yes, Barky," Trenton snapped. "Tests. Do you think we would just look at it with awe and wonder?"

"Perhaps you," I replied and noted Vanderguud stifling a smile behind his hand which he now spread to cover his lower face.

Trenton shook off the snide remark, raised his hand, hesitated then followed through by running his hand across the side of his head. I could see him simmering.

"What tests did this item defy?" I asked.

"The x-ray revealed nothing, but a blank blob." Allister had sit stoically at the table with his hands neatly folded in front of him. Now, he seemed more animated. "Our attempts to view the inside of the cylinder were just feeble stabs in the dark, it was impervious to our studies. A drop of acid was carefully administered to it, but the acid rolled off with absolutely no damage. We used varying strengths of fire and considered sending it through a local crematorium." He stopped and smiled. "We didn't do that for fear if it did indeed burn, we'd lose it. Still, the item wasn't damaged in any manner with the gamut of tests including water, freezing and the rest."

"Did anyone attempt the obvious?" I asked and leaned forward to rest my hands on the table before me. Their blank expressions told me they had no idea what I meant.

"A hammer?" I was amused. "Brute force?"

A loud sigh of disgust was Trenton's response. Vanderguud smiled openly.

"Yes," the man sitting at the opposite end from Trenton quipped. He sheepishly smiled at me. "I gently tapped the dang thing with a hammer and then progressively gained force." He sat there innocently watching me.

"And?" I asked.

"It was very frustrating." The man spread his hands before him on the table. "And yet it was quite exhilarating." His eyes twinkled at the memory. "No matter how hard I hit the cylinder, there wasn't a mark on it. I even put it into a vise which broke under the stress." He paused. "The vice broke, not the cylinder."

"Basically, Dr. Havens." Vanderguud once more took control of the conversation. "This item appears to be almost indestructible."

I leaned forward. "Interesting, may I see it again?"

This time I was scrutinizing over its surface searching for any indication of abuse. There was nothing to see but my frowning expression reflecting back at me. I shook the container again, closed my eyes and let the moment embrace me.

"Definitely not heavy," Allister said. "My assumption aligns with yours, Dr. Havens. It is probably some type of soft material inside, perhaps silk."

"It could be a dumb feather for all we know," Trenton quipped.

"No," I said, correcting Trenton. "It's definitely not a feather. If it were, the calamus, the shaft's tip, if you will, would make a small tapping sound as it lifted and fell. Whatever this is, it is soft and I am making a very general guess, possibly pliant. Perhaps it is nothing more than wadded up spider webs, sealed for all eternity inside this cylinder waiting for the technology to open it and weave the fine silken strands into clothing."

"Peter!" Trenton huffed. "Are you going to accept this type of mystic crap?"

"Mysticism, Trenton?" Vanderguud replied. "Perhaps I'm mesmerized by Dr. Havens' knowledge, but I'm definitely not mystified by Dr. Havens' manners."

I nodded my head to acknowledge Vanderguud's compliment.

Vanderguud clapped his hands. "Gentlemen, are we in agreement?"

"Well, I'm not," Trenton snarled. He sat there with his arms defiantly folded across his chest. "I really believe there are better choices than this bungling charlatan before us."

"I agree with you Trent, he wasn't our first choice." Vanderguud ignored me sitting in front of him. "Still, he is available and seems to have a solid knowledge base. Do you agree or not?"

I kept my face as emotionless as possible. Trenton was getting called on the carpet. He either had to put up or shut up.

"Barclay's talents seem to work even though they are rather unusual," Trenton admitted. "If the board is adamant about hiring him and if he is willing to take the assignment, then I have one additional condition or request."

"A request?" Vanderguud echoed.

"I want to join the expedition to keep a watch on our investment."

I wasn't sure about Trenton going with me and I silently watched Vanderguud scan his associates for assurances.

"We wouldn't have it any other way," Vanderguud stated. "Am I correct, gentlemen?"

I noticed Trenton's facial expression change. I truly believe he thought they wouldn't bow to his demands. I quickly noted the expressions of the remaining board members and I realized Trenton had walked into their trap. They had called his bluff and were pleased by the thought of him not being around. Of course, I wasn't too thrilled about the resulting outcome, the prospect of him joining me. This also let me know I wasn't messing with an amateur. Vanderguud could make a solid opponent.

I leaned on the table and spun the artifact on its axis. *Spin the bottle*, I thought, *and where it lands, nobody knows.*

"Anybody got an estimated age? How old do you think this thing is?" I asked.

"Ah, yes, Dr. Havens," The gentlemen on the opposite end from Trenton lifted a hand into the air. "Exactly how old do you think it is?"

I felt the right side of my lips curl up in a grin. "Off hand, I'd guess no less than ten years, at best. More likely, it probably came from the future since I can't think of any technology that is as good as this item appears." I frowned and stared at the cylinder. "You said the stone was thousands of years old," I muttered. "If the cylinder actually was a part of the rock at its inception, then that would indicate it is also at least that age."

The man nodded. "As I'm sure you are aware, Dr. Havens, using carbon dating is only accurate to approximately sixty thousand years ago."

"Your point being, Dr..." My mind was blank as to this gentleman's name.

"Dr. James Farwell." He snickered. "I was watching your consternation when you were introduced to Trenton. I could tell you were trying to recall where you knew him from and our names were literally passing above you, unheard."

"My apologies." I hoped the heat I felt in my cheeks didn't brighten them too red. "You're very astute and correct."

"You probably don't remember me, either, but we were in a class together during your junior year." Farwell smiled. "Seems like old home week, doesn't it, Dr. Havens?"

"I'm afraid you have me at a disadvantage," I replied.

"It's really immaterial." Farwell waved his hand to dismiss the comment. "Back to that which is important, the artifact. We attempted carbon dating without success and had to use Uranium-235, to which I was able to get a reading."

I waited. There was absolute silence of the room. Why the delay?

"And?" I finally asked.

"Dr. Havens." Farwell slid an open hand across his temple. "The test said that it was over 500 million years old."

"You mean 500 thousand," I replied.

"No, I stated million. I said 500 million."

I watched the man as he nervously shook his head as if that were to convince me. His voice trembled in stress.

"You obviously re-tested." I fidgeted as the truth of the anomaly reached and tore at my gut.

"Yes," he replied. There was a hesitation. "Actually, we performed it several more times with different methods including potassium-40, argon-40, argon-39 and thermoluminescence dating on the object."

"And your results were?" I offered.

Dr. Farwell appeared he was going to have a nervous breakdown. His hands, fingers splayed out in front of him, shook and his mouth moved but no sounds came out. Finally, he appeared to crack and began to start giggling like a fool.

"Dr. Farwell," Vanderguud shouted. "Control yourself. You're a scientific scholar."

"Yes," Farwell replied. "Yes, I am." He inhaled deeply, wiped a tear from his eye, and released the breath while jerking his head in an attempt to remove a possible kink.

"All of the tests revealed the cylinder to be over 500 million years old," he said. "This thing is older than most of our continents." He hesitated. "Think Pan—"

"Your thoughts?" Vanderguud interrupted and smiled at me.

I sat there thinking—500 million years. That would be in direct correlation to the granite.

"Did you happen to check the age of the stone?" I asked.

Trenton huffed loudly. "Yes, Barclay. We checked. It is approximately 375 million years old."

"Therein is one of the quandaries," Vanderguud added.

"Now what do you think?" Trenton asked. There was a renewed smugness about him that I just wanted to go up to him and slap his face.

I was about to reply to Trenton's snide remark when Vanderguud's single word sank in: quandaries.

"Exactly how many quandaries do you have?" I asked.

"This particular item has several." Vanderguud lifted his hand. "Age, material, location, contents." With each word, a finger lifted to denote the count.

"We've addressed the contents earlier," I said. "Age is what we're discussing now and I agree that something this apparently new shouldn't be stuck in something as old as that stone chunk."

"You mean something that old stuck in something as young as that stone chunk." Trenton narrowed his eyes to glare at me. "You seemed to have forgotten the metal artifact is older than the stone."

"No," I replied. Trying to ignore him was going to be difficult, but having him on the expedition was going to be real hell. "You said material and location were also problems?"

"Material," Allister started. "We were able to discern some of the metals but there are some very unique items we've not been able to decipher even with using a spectrograph."

"Interesting," I said.

"That was deep," Trenton muttered.

"Trenton," Vanderguud snapped. He stood facing the younger man, his fingers were curled into fists as he leaned on the table with his knuckles. "One more outburst of that caliber and I'll physically have you removed from this room. Your petty sophomoric routines will not be tolerated any longer. Am I understood?"

Trenton eased back into his chair, folded his arms over his chest, and grimaced to display utter disregard. It made me feel good. I was seeing how to get the best of him.

"You mentioned location," I started. "Exactly what do you mean by that?"

"That's another of the enigmas of this item," Baxter said. He had a small smile on his face and I could tell he was probably thrilled by Vanderguud's call at Trenton. "The item was purchased at a village market in Brazil but the granite is not indigenous to Brazil's central area but the western extreme. Then, of course, there is the lava."

"I noticed it," I offered. "Not typical mixture."

"We did a bit of research," Baxter replied.

"Hmrph!" mumbled Trenton to which Vanderguud shot him a glare.

"Alright, an extreme amount of research to locate a match on the lava," Baxter spat. "The only place this lava could have come from was the island of Principe, in the Atlantic Ocean, off the western coast of Africa." Once more he hesitated. "Only in the Pangaean Era would the continents have been relatively close to mix these two items." He paused. "I'm referring to the granite and lava."

Vanderguud scowled at Baxter.

I looked at the five men, then at the artifact lying between Vanderguud and me. Pangaea. The concept tickled my bones and I got a warm fuzzy as I visualized a globe with clear, blue oceans and only one major continent. Pangaea. My mind raced with ideas of how these two items, the stone and the cylinder, came to be connected.

"Are you still with us?" Vanderguud tapped the table to catch my attention.

"I'll consider the expedition," I finally said while nodding my head at the five men opposite me. "I would appreciate a small amount of time to examine the item at my apartment." I looked at the group. "If that is acceptable," I quickly added.

There was a quick mumbling and whispering among the four men. I noticed Trenton had been left out of and he didn't seem to mind.

"Fine, Dr. Havens." Vanderguud stood. "The object, the Cylinder of Time, as we call it, belongs to Reverend Thompson. We will notify him you have it in your possession. I am sure Jacob or Ronald will convey the message."

There was a small pause of silence and Dr. Vanderguud glanced at the young men sitting behind me.

Vanderguud glanced at his companions. "Shall we re-convene tomorrow, say about nine thirty in the morning?"

Everyone nodded their heads in agreement except Trenton who remained aloof.

"Thank you, Dr. Havens, for your time," Vanderguud said. He leaned over the table and shook my hand again. "Let me see you to the door."

I reached down and grabbed the cylinder and stone from the table.

"Keep that protected at all times, Barky," Trenton warned and threw a cloth for me to wrap around the relics. "You don't want to piss off Reverend Thompson."

The young woman who had sat at the back of the room smiled politely at me as I walked out of the room. Her companion had given me the chair. He nodded, yet had an apprehensive expression.

Curious, they had been in the room the whole time and never once joined the conversation.

End of Sample Read...

www.ingramcontent.com/pod-product-compliance
Lightning Source LLC
Chambersburg PA
CBHW070841310526
45793CB00010B/161